SELF-REALIZATION, SUCCESS, AND ADJUSTMENT

SELF-REALIZATION, SUCCESS, AND ADJUSTMENT

Edited by
Edgar Krau

PRAEGER

New York
Westport, Connecticut
London

Library of Congress Cataloging-in-Publication Data

Self-realization, success, and adjustment.

   Includes bibliographies and index.
   1. Self-realization. 2. Success. 3. Adjustment
(Psychology) I. Krau, Edgar.
BF637.S4S45   1989   158'.1   88–30747
ISBN 0–275–93210–9 (alk. paper)

Library of Congress Catalog Card Number: 88–30747
ISBN: 0–275–93210–9

First published in 1989

Praeger Publishers, One Madison Avenue, New York, NY 10010
A division of Greenwood Press, Inc.

Printed in the United States of America

The paper used in this book complies with the Permanent
Paper Standard issued by the National Information Standards
Organization (Z39.48–1984)

10 9 8 7 6 5 4 3 2 1

Hamlet: What is a man,
If his chief good and market of his time
Be that to sleep and feed?
a beast, no more

               [Shakespeare]

Only man alone	Nur allein der Mensch
Can do the impossible.	Vermag das Unmögliche
He can decide	Er unterscheidet
He chooses and judges,	Wählet und richtet;
Can give the moment	Er kann dem Augenblick
Lasting endurance.	Dauer verleihen
[Goethe, *The Godlike*,	[Goethe: *Das Göttliche*]
Transl. E. H. Zeydel, 1955]	

I raise a voice for far superber themes for poets and for art
. . .
To teach the average man the glory of his daily walk and trade,
. . .
For every man to see that he really do something, for every woman, too.
          [Walt Whitman, *Song of the Exposition*]

Contents

Illustrations

Preface

Since the early 1970s it has become clear that changes are taking place in people's values: the material values of the industrial society of competition are being replaced by the values of the post-industrial society centering on self-development and self-realization. What is going on has not only theoretical importance and concerns not only the spiritual élite of society; there is mounting pressure even from the modest social strata to recognize their right to self-realization. The existing self-realization theories are pyramidal *qua* élitist: no access to self-realization before the person succeeds in satisfying the lower-order materialistic needs. In a period of chronic economic difficulties this amounts to the delegitimization of the possibility of self-realization for the ordinary man. The book will argue that the existing pyramidal self-realization theories linking self-actualization to success in competition for wealth and honors are not only unfair according to modern society's new ethics, they are also indefensible in the light of a deeper scientific analysis of the phenomenon. In the present book this analysis is performed on a multilateral basis by an international group of authors. They examine the historical roots of the problem, the theoretical aspects of a new theory on self-realization, and the practical problems of implementation. Although in principle people do not need a theoretical framework to actualize themselves, a good theory certainly enhances the process.

Part I of the book analyzes the meaning of self-realization for the modern man: Is it success? Is it money or the access to power? Is it the challenge of work? As a conclusion to these analyses a new theory of self-realization will be put forward defining self-realization in the framework of adjustment.

Part II gives a theoretical and practical analysis of the means to achieving self-realization: participation behavior in the social process ensuring the feeling of individual causation and of psychological property; the development of self-concept and of cognitive, affective, and motivational characteristics of the personality; the planning and planful realization of life-long careers; and above all the plan project of one's life. A separate chapter deals with the self-realization of modern women. Finally, the discussion extends to coping with the blocking of self-realization by crises, stress, and anxiety. The chapters in Part II contain suggestions regarding counseling for self-realization.

PART I
The Meaning of Self-Realization

1

The Old–New Problem
of Self-Realization:
The Lessons of History

Edgar Krau

We are told every day that change is the central problem of our society. Technology and the sciences of man are focusing their main preoccupations on supporting, keeping up, and furthering the challenges and opportunities created by the rapidly changing frameworks of material and social existence. The striving for self-realization in men and women is a powerful motive force for change. We may accept or we may be critical of the Marxian thesis stating that while transforming nature, man transforms himself (Marx and Engels, *Die deutsche Ideologie*); the fact remains that there is a link between our own transformation and our interaction with the environment. Nobody can deny the dialectical character of the process in which cause and effect are continually changing their place and role.

The paramount philosophical and social importance of self-realization as a motivating force lies in the assumption that it is presumed to produce modifications for the better. This conviction may again be open to discussion. More than 200 years ago, in his brilliant pamphlet *Discours sur les sciences et les arts,* Rousseau put forward the thesis that the development of material civilization, achieved through the efforts of many talented people, has not contributed to the improvement of customs and morality. Giving a wrong interpretation to its positivist and experimentalist credo, modern society generally ignores the problem; but can we afford to do so? If self-realization is nothing less *and* nothing more than the full realization of one's potential once all one's needs have been fully satisfied, as the positivist conception would hold, then at the height of their power Idi-Amin of Uganda or Emperor Bocassa of Central Africa would have been models of self-realization to be followed by every human being. I intentionally give these examples to avoid any ideological arguments on present figures of power, but the reader will readily be able to find an entire gallery of tyrants in various positions and geographical places who are not deposed, and not sentenced to death (as is the case with Bocassa), but wreck existences and take human lives in actualizing all their potential and fulfilling all their needs.

Why do we ignore this problem that has been raised by human thought? Our positivist experimentalist science of man generally ignores all that is not contemporary. We are accustomed to label as obsolete all that has been produced over the centuries by the most noble and excellent minds. This is a mistake. It impoverishes our horizons and the content of our arguments and discussions.

The history of human thought has not only contributed moral considerations to the clarification of the problem of self-realization. We shall document the thesis that only by taking into account the tremendous richness of thought invested by the human mind in this problem are experiments able to address the right questions, are the experimenters able to give the right interpretation to their findings. In this introductory chapter, we shall discuss the lessons to be learned from reviewing the preoccupations of centuries of human meditation on man's self-realization.

There are numerous aspects imposing the necessity of searching for a new approach to the problem of self-realization; the already indicated moral aspect is only one of them. As a matter of fact, it is linked to the broader question of who has the right to determine whether an individual has attained self-realization—society, the individual himself? And if it is the latter, is there the possibility of establishing scientific criteria? Above all, is self-realization a real possibility or an unattainable ideal? If it is a real possibility, does it exist for everybody? If not, what are the inhibiting factors, can they be overcome, and if so, how? What are the areas of self-realization? Is it only the domain of work, as well-known modern theorists used to think (Maslow, 1954; Alderfer, 1969)? What about women's self-realization? Is self-realization an achievement for all time, or has it a temporary character, and then what are the rules of its evolution? At present the answers to these questions are not satisfactory. A new approach to the problem is not a superfluous luxury of ideas; it is a necessity.

In search of a new approach to the self-realization problem, one paradoxically has to start with the wisdom of ages, but avoid its fallacies. The reason for this has been indicated. Self-realization is not a new task, nor is it a problem that appeared only as a result of scientific, economic, and technological progress. What is new is only the greater complexity of the problem and the multiple possibilities of choice open to the individual on the path of actualizing his/her potential. What should also be new is the democratization of self-realization by recognizing that it is not the prerogative of merely a few chosen people.

What meanings have been given to self-realization throughout history? In *Charmides*, one of his early dialogues, Plato deals with the problems of wisdom in man. The characters are youths—beautiful youths. Socrates, the leading figure in almost all of Plato's dialogues, confesses that all young people seem beautiful to him because in all of them there is the promise of "the other beauty"—wisdom. There is no final definition of wisdom in this dialogue, but it is suggested that wisdom lies in knowing yourself as you are able to differentiate between Good and Evil. Already here, at the dawn of human thought on self-perfection, it is stressed that the "promise of wisdom" lies in everyone and that it is linked to the moral dilemma. Plato put strong emphasis on this Socratian idea. Knowledge for him meant virtue, the striving toward virtue. The latter is neglected only because it is not known. Otherwise its brightness is so overwhelming that knowing virtue, we are necessarily inclined to follow it. Knowledge brings man closer to perfection, not merely from a moral point of view. For Plato the philosopher, only absolute ideas have real existence. A flower is beautiful because it participates in the absolute idea of beauty. Wisdom is moral and beautiful, and therefore love loves wisdom. Its aim is to procreate in beauty and make beauty be ours forever.

It is a pity that when speaking of more actual events, Plato renounces many of his lofty ideas. In his *Republic* there is no longer any mention of equal promises of wisdom and beauty lying in everyone. The estates of society express the divine intention: "The magistrates of the state will tell the youth that God who created them, mixed gold in the making of those capable of ruling, and therefore they are more valuable. He mixed silver in the composition of warriors, iron and bronze in the composition of peasants and of craftsmen." "Will they be happy?" ask the participants in the dialogue. "Not their well-being is the concern, but the state's," replies Plato. Does not this remind us of very familiar contemporary tunes? Furthermore, this gold–silver–iron illustration evokes associations with a well-known modern system of pyramidal need gratification. It does not matter that in our modern world there is no longer the word of God (alas!), but that of socioeconomic conditions, hereditary limitations, and so forth. Incidentally, in Plato's view the peasant and the warrior were able to attain the measure of perfection preestablished for them, whereas in our modern conception we concede self-realization only for the top of the social pyramid. Even here the ancient world seems closer to fairness and truth.

It is in these "concrete" social matters that Plato is complemented by his otherwise unfaithful disciple, Aristotle. For the latter, existence is comprised of individual things and ideas; categories are merely their abstraction. Aristotle therefore does not speak of an ideal man, but of the man of his time. The purpose of human activity is happiness which is attained through virtue, but on this point Aristotle comes close to his "master." The moral ideal varies according to social conditions and individual possibilities—for some this ideal is in honor, for others in wealth or in science—but Aristotle declares that there is a certain measure of virtue and happiness in every social estate. A poor man cannot be generous, and if he were, he would be a fool. Man's position in society is innate, and equality reigns only between equals. For people who are not equal, inequality is just and fair. Some doctrines of today are less outspoken, but the sense is the same. From this point of view, there is no relief in Aristotle; he remained a prisoner of his time. However, if we look at the class of equals, the free citizens of Athens, Aristotle makes a very important contribution to the problems raised by the theory of self-realization.

First, Aristotle states that happiness, as the highest good, is fully attainable. Virtue and pleasure are both good in themselves; however, they are chosen for the sake of happiness, while happiness is never chosen for their sake. Happiness has no separate and independent existence. Were it so, it could not be achieved or attained by man. But the happiness man is concerned with *is* attainable (*Ethica Nicomachea*)

Second, Aristotle links happiness with man's activity, and this contradicts the Stoics, and later the conception of St. Augustine and St. Thomas Aquinas, who considered happiness a state of the soul. Aristotle defines happiness as an activity of the soul in accordance with virtue (here we have again the moral point of view forgotten today!), and if there is more than one virtue, it is an activity in accordance with the best and most complete virtue in a complete life (*Ethica Nicomachea*). This definition leads to two further important points. One of them is that virtuous activity leads to happiness only if it has importance also for others and not only for the individual himself. Happy is the individual who achieves something for his parents, for his children, for his wife, and in general for his friends and fellow citizens, since man is born for citizenship. Our modern world has definitely much to learn from Aristotle. When Maslow (1954) defines the self-realizing person as a "happy animal, full of lust," the purpose and content of behavior is hardly the well-being of friends and fellow citizens.

The second point in Aristotle's definition of happiness is that it follows from a *complete* life. This is very important, and one could see here a prefiguration of the full need gratification thesis. Unfortunately, Aristotle's interpretation supports such a view, as he contends that there must be enough external goods and good fortune to enable a man to live out his life in some leisure and dignity. "For one swallow does not make a summer, nor does one day; and so too, one day, or a short time does not make a man blessed and happy" (*Ethica Nicomachea*). It is here that the critique of Aristotle was most severe and that one thousand years of philosophical–psychological thinking turned away from him. St. Augustine's "Do not go outward, inward is the truth" (Augustinus, *De Trinitate*) lighted the way not only for neo-Platonians, but for all who saw happiness in moral and aesthetical perfection: it will be the "amor dei intellectualis" of Spinoza, and

Schiller's aesthetical perfection. Even for Epicurus—and this contrary to the general perception of his ideas—the pleasures of the soul are the most lasting. In the letter to Menoikes, he writes: "When we are saying that pleasure is the supreme good, we are not thinking of hunting the pleasures of senses, but of preventing the suffering of soul and body." In his *Ethics* he continues this thought and points out that the pleasures derived from friendship and knowledge are the most lasting. Happy is the one who leaves this world without anger; "happy is the sage living on bread and water but his is the pleasure of the supreme good: the serenity of the mind."

This does not mean that, from the point of view of today's scientists, Aristotle is wrong or that Epicurus, Spinoza, or Augustine are. They simply refer to different kinds of persons. We should not think that despising "worldly goods" is idle philosophical talk. Those people lived accordingly. Spinoza rejected the legacy bequeathed by his parents, the pension offered to him by Louis XIV of France, and the philosophy chair at the University of Heidelberg offered by the Palatine Elector. He lived a hard life and died of consumption at the age of 45. Philosophy was the pleasure of his life, and for its sake he refused all honors and material benefits. Epicurus was not a wealthy man either; nor was he healthy. He lived like a hermit without ever marrying. Was he happy? A short time before his death he wrote to his friend, Hermarchos: "I am writing you at the end of a happy day of my life. My disease is cruel and pain is so violent that it is therefore not capable of growing. I am fighting pain and illness with the joy which fills my heart when I remember the talks we had together."

Now the solution of the problem seems at hand, and we discuss it at length in Chapter 4. For self-realization (and happiness) to occur, life has to provide the "quality" important to the person, and this prevents him/her from being unhappy and feeling miserable (the "sufferings of soul and body"). There remains the problem of duration in happiness ("one day does not make a man blessed and happy").

First, our problem is that of self-realization; happiness is a state that accompanies and results from self-realization. There are great differences between people from the point of view of the period during and in which they achieved maximum self-realization. Goethe finished his Faust at the age of 82, having spent decades working on his masterpiece, the apex of his poetical work; by the age of 19, the French poet Rimbaud (1854–1891) had already written all of his work that enjoyed great success and had considerable influence on French literature. Rimbaud lived 18 years more, the mean life of an adventurer. His achievements and creative enthusiasm referred to a very short period.

Second, introducing the prerequisite of duration of happiness simply makes the problem unsolvable. The example above illustrates this point, but perhaps a better one is Aristotle himself. From all that is known, he was not happy in his last years. He had a stomach illness that sounds like an ulcer to the modern ear—and this is obviously not an illness stemming from too much happiness. Besides, there is the famous and mysterious story of his death: he fell into the sea from a cliff on the island of Euboia. One rumor has it that he feared that his "fellow citizens" were preparing for him the same fate they had bestowed upon Socrates. Be that as it may, the final unhappiness of Aristotle is an argument against his theory but not against his achieved self-realization—the great thinker wrote about 400 books on all issues of philosophy and science known in his day and influenced thought for centuries. Nor is it an argument against his happiness at various peak points of his life.

As such, it is wrong to set time requirements for the duration of self-realization and happiness. Panta rei—"all is changing"—is the adage attributed to Heraclitus. He said: "one cannot step twice into the same river" (Heraclitus, *Fragments*). What is understood is that the individual is no longer the same person when he comes to bathe a second time. Heraclitus convinces us that we should not look for everlasting things in human life—including happiness, including self-realization, we may add. In this book we discuss a solution that takes into account the dialectical aspects of life when dealing with self-realization.

For the moment let us see what followed from the development of the Aristotelian conception of happiness. Happiness, says Kant in his *Critique of Pure Reason*, "is the satisfaction of all our desires; extensive in regard to their multiplicity; intensive in regard to their degree; protensive in regard to their duration," and in his *Critique of Practical Reason* he states in detail what he means by happiness: power, riches, honor, even health, and a general well-being and contentment with one's condition. Although this definition is unilateral because there is no mention of achievements in the spiritual realm (mentioned in other places), it has substantial importance; first, because it underlines the link between happiness and self-realization (in honors, riches, etc.), and, second, because it includes contentment with one's condition among the characteristics of happiness. For the psychological theory of self-realization we shall conclude at this stage that there can be no self-realization without happiness and no happiness without contentment with one's condition.

Kant has not Aristotle's moderation. For the latter, virtue is always the middle way. Kant draws the ultimate conclusions from every position. In Kant's view not only is happiness desired, but it is necessarily desired—and never attained, for it is unlikely that any man could get through life with all his desires maximally satisfied and with no interruption of such maximal satisfaction. Kant does not state what *is* actually attained and if what is being attained is still self-realization and happiness as it had been defined. Psychologically, the idea of a maximal all-comprehensive, everlasting satisfaction of desires leads to a dead end.

Progress has been possible in directions of thought concentrating on man's real life, and not on ideal states. Such directions focus on the explicit link between happiness and self-realization, or even on self-realization alone as Descartes does. As he himself puts it, he breaks with all opinions and theories he had learned and tries to reconstruct from its foundations his system of knowledge (Descartes, *Discourse de la méthode*). For a philosopher, his first conclusion is completely surprising: "La conservation de la santé est le premier bien" [the preservation of health is the first good of all] and the basis for all other goals, because the mind depends so much on the temperament and the disposition of the organs that, if it is possible to find some means that might make men more wise and able, one should look for it in medicine. More than two centuries later, H. Spencer in *The Data of Ethics* will say the same thing.

The four rules Descartes established for the conduct of his life refer to self-realization: to choose the most convenient occupation for the cultivation of the mind; to work so as to overcome himself rather than luck, to modify his desires rather than change the world order, and to convince himself that nothing is more in one's power than one's thoughts; to submit to the laws and customs of his country; to be decisive and firm in his deeds, and to follow even doubtful opinions if he resolved to accept them.

The central idea that follows from these rules is important. It shows that for self-realization to be achieved one has to be decisive, persevering, and flexible as one submits to laws, customs, and existing conditions. Descartes does not clarify to which laws to submit and against which to stand up to and be decided and firm (he himself was forced to live in Holland because of his opinions), but a most valuable idea is that without some sort of adjustment no self-realization is possible. We return to this idea in Chapter 4. Meanwhile let us take a look at how self-realization is seen by Spinoza.

As also for Descartes, in Spinoza's conception man lives to maintain his existence on earth; there is no use in meditating on death and on the beyond: "eius sapientia non mortis sed vitae meditatio est" (*Ethica*). However, we are able to maintain our existence only following the principles of life shown by reason. At this point Spinoza apparently turns toward an élitist conception of self-realization. The mob is not capable of living according to the principles of reason; to believe so is a poetical dream of times gone. Life teaches that what people really value are three things: riches, honors, and bodily pleasure. Only a few are capable of finding God through knowledge—those who found Him before they had sought (as St. Augustine said, "I sought because I found").

If we deepen the analysis of these ideas from the point of view of a psychologist, we may find here an interesting hidden conception. Since preservation of life is the supreme good, self-realization in a preserved (good) life may be possible for anyone who attains the three things praised by the mob; but in the philosopher Spinoza's view, this is an inferior kind of self-realization. The superior, true self-realization corresponding to Spinoza's moral credo (it is characteristic that these ideas on self-realization appear in his treatise entitled *Ethica*) includes the ascension to the finding of God—and of this only a few chosen are capable. Using modern terminology, it would be appropriate to give this conception also an additional interpretation: self-realization is possible in a number of areas. From a moral point of view some are superior, and they ought to be regarded as the true areas of self-realization. Understandably, Spinoza is concerned with the latter. Riches and honors cannot satisfy us because we never have enough of them, and pleasures are often accompanied by bitterness because they are transient. It appears that in Spinoza's theory of self-realization, a particular emphasis is given to the restraint of our passions, which, since they are based on confused ideas, direct our behavior into inappropriate avenues. Ordinary people are the slaves of their passions. In a significant way, Spinoza entitles the chapter of *Ethica* dealing with human passions "De servitute hominis". Without liberation from the tyranny of our passions, no self-realization is possible.

It is important to note that by passion Spinoza means confused ideas. A century later d'Holbach will lay the foundations for dividing emotions and sentiments from a moral point of view. "We approve the interests of people whenever they result in an advantage for the human species," he points out in his *Système de la nature*. "Therefore we approve courage, the love of liberty and virtue, but not in a disinterested way because habit and reflection have given us the moral sense and the aesthetical taste. . . . We should destroy harmful passions by the aid of those which are useful to society."

Using this interpretation of morality, it is convenient to divide sentiments and passions into morally superior and inferior ones. As to the morally inferior sentiments, they indeed prevent self-realization if, as already agreed, we relate them to an ethical point of view. Conversely, superior sentiments are necessary conditions for any major achievement—the way Cajal puts it in his book addressed to young scientists: "every great achievement in arts as well as in science is the result of a great passion serving a great idea" (Cajal, 1923).

Since morality is not innate (d'Holbach says, "the arm nature gave me is neither good or bad, it becomes criminal using it for murder"), the moral premises for self-realization lie in everyone if we talk of the possibility of restraining our passions. This is the position of Descartes (*Traité des passions*): "Il n' y a point d'âme si faible qu'elle ne puisse acquérir un pouvoir absolu sur ses passions"; and it contradicts Spinoza's thesis that only a spiritual élite is capable of having power over their passions. Even if it is physiologically not true that "there is no soul so weak as not to be able to acquire absolute power over its passions"—we think, for instance, of drug addition—Descartes' position is more in line with a conception of self-realization that does not restrict the phenomenon to a few chosen people.

This problem of natural endowment is of substantial importance for setting the framework of action for the self-realization phenomenon. It is a kind of iron law for Leibniz (*Discourse on Metaphysics*) derived from the logical principle of "praedicatum inest subiecto." He writes: "Nobody can teach us anything if the idea is not already in our mind as a material from which the thought is formed." Even Diderot, in his rejection of Helvetius' book, *L'Hommme (Réfutations)*, contends that the natural organization of the brain separates the genius from the imbecile, and the man nature has chosen for a certain function (sic!) is different from the one who thinks only of work, attention, passion. The problem is whether only the genius is capable of self-realization or also the latter category. Nietzsche, in *Der Wille zur Macht*, opts for the genius, the strong, uncommon man. He opts for transforming the strong, powerful man into superman as he counterposes him to the image of the doomed, lost man. The difference between them is mainly in their moral profile, wherein superman is no longer bound by any convention or moral limitation. Nietzsche's morality rests on power.

Three points in Nietzsche's conception are of concern to our discussion. First, its idealistic character. Nietzsche knows it and recognizes it by not outlining any concrete plan for reaching the stage of superman. In the second place, the emphasis of the will, the striving toward the ideal of power, of superman underlines the psychological function of striving, of potentiality for improvement. It could be a meritorious thought were it not linked to the superman image. The power philosophy of Nietzsche—and this is our third point—makes superman crush all social conventions, including the state—the "coldest of all monsters," as Nietzsche calls it. "Can we be still content with the man of the present day?" Nietzsche's Zarathustra asks, and he answers: "Another ideal hovers before our eyes. . . . It is an ideal of a spirit to whom the highest popular standards would be mere danger, a decay, an abasement, a temporary forgetfulness of self" (*Thus Spake Zarathustra*). Such a self-realized superman is an ideal that obviously cannot be attained and thus marks the dead end of maximalistic demands for self-realization, the plight of the idea that self-realization is achieved only by geniuses and supermen. Those who attempted a self-styled "application" of these ideas degenerated into mass murderers. Examples are far too well known to insist on them.

If, however, one is to remain inside the framework of society and of social conventions the problem, even that of geniuses, is whether there is a general consensus regarding achievements of even moral values. Thomas Hobbes, the great pessimist of the seventeenth century, responded negatively. He too (as Nietzsche two centuries later) saw in the will toward power a main moving force. It is man's main passion, and therefore there is no generally accepted aim or sense of the good which unifies people. The different constitution of the individuals, their prejudices, passions, interests and subjective dispositions, contribute to the different colors in which concepts like virtue, wisdom, and justice appear to people (Hobbes, *De Homine, Leviathan*). Hobbes sees no superior common goal that could lead to a common human solidarity. Everyone strives to realize his desires at the expense of others: *Homo homini lupus*. If two people desire a certain thing that only one of them can have, they fight until one subdues the other or they are both destroyed. The only possibility is to reduce the adversary to a state in which the latter can no longer appear as a threat. The natural state of mankind is war, and only because such a state does not guarantee anyone's life do people have to restrict their liberty.

Did we not know that these words were written in the seventeenth century, we would think that we are hearing a lecture on the ways to self-realization in our modern achievement society, albeit with one difference: our modern lecturer would be less outspoken and would hide behind theories of natural endowment and personality types. Hobbes was more sincere. He points out that people are equal in nature, in the sense that from the point of view of bodily force, even the weakest has enough power to kill the strongest if he uses appropriate means.

Is this the meaning of self-realization? The full actualization of Jack the Ripper's, Henrich Himmler's, or Al Capone's potential? The omission of the moral point of view in defining self-realization leads to a second dead end. This situation is recognized by Freud, who denies altogether the possibility of self-realization and of happiness in modern society, allegedly because of the limitations society's ethics impose on the possibility of man actualizing his instinctive drives. The latter are, par excellence, contrary to the moral barriers erected by society. In "Das Unbehagen in der Kultur,"Freud points out that happiness is not a cultural value. There is always the need to subordinate happiness to the discipline of work in a full-time job, to the discipline of monogamic reproduction, and to the system of established law and order. Culture means the systematic sacrifice of the libido, its constrained deflection to a socially useful expression. Our society is, by its nature, a repressive one, and people are entitled to ask for happiness only if this is defined in congruence with the existing values. However, in doing so, the very values of happiness are repressed. In a study on philosophical anthropology, Fromm (1972) sees Freud's equation as "gratification of instincts but barbaric, or their partial repression and spiritual development." For the latter, man pays the price of neurosis.

It should be mentioned that when Freud sees in civilization the negation of self-realization and happiness, he is referring to civilization as such, not just to its modern form! Freud's outlook on history is pessimistic: man is not capable of freeing himself from the tragic alternative to destroy either himself or others (Fromm, 1972). Hobbes' "Homo homini lupus" adage receives an unexpected support from depth psychology.

Nevertheless, man is *essentially* a *zoön politikon*, a social animal, as Aristotle has seen him. There is no natural "free" state outside society or before it came into being. Human beings have been found in forests or in the jungle, brought up by animals and living as animals in adaptation to this environment. None of these people was able to return to life in the society of fellow men. Edgar Burrough's Tarzan tales are very attractive, but they are just tales. All manifestations of man's social life bear a sociohistorical conditioning. Self-realization and happiness may be easier in some social structures and more difficult in others, but since it has been observed in many people, it is in principle possible. The question that arises is, of course, which are the features of social life giving broader possibilities to self-realization and the accompanying feeling of happiness? We try to answer this question in the following chapters.

What seems certain is that our modern Western society, even in its form of "consumption society," is far from fostering the feeling of self-fulfillment in its members. It is not a mere coincidence that precisely in our time there is a tremendous increase in the strength and the spreading of most pessimistic philosophies such as existentialist ones.

The idea of self-realization is central to the existentialist schools of thought as they advocate the acquisition of an "authentic" mode of life, which would liberate the human being from the impersonal day-to-day existence in a world characterized by mediocrity, vulgarity, frequency. In such a world there is no self, and man disappears as an individual (Jaspers, 1960). We enjoy what all enjoy, we read, contemplate, judge literature and art like all do. In our day-to-day life we therefore appear not as acting subjects but as an object performing the actions imposed by man's commonality (Heidegger, 1957).

Existentialism is not a philosophy of social improvement. The edge of the criticism is directed against the contemporary world, but it is contended that its negative features are inherent in all human existence—an absurd one which has no cause and no end, save death. Every one of us finds himself here, now—why not in another place, in another time—it is absurd. However, at this precise point the existentialist philosophers see man's great chance: to be for death. "To look in the face of death every moment of my life is my unique chance to escape from the impersonal mediocrity and to become a personality, to live an authentic existence. Man becomes thus conscious that his existence is his sole responsibility; he becomes free and the master of his world" (Sartre, 1946). "To live intensively," writes Marcel (1963), "means to be exposed in a twofold sense: to external influences and to the person's confrontations, it means the courage to expose oneself." To live a personal life means to involve oneself with the situation and with new responsibilities, it means to steadily surpass the acquired situation. There is no illusion as to the final outcome. All our work is comparable to that of the mythological Sisyphus doomed by the gods endlessly to carry a rock to the top of a mountain, from where the rock will inevitably fall back. But Sisyphus is free and happy. There is no fate so bad that it cannot be overcome by despising it (Camus, 1942). The either–or of man on his road to self-realization is, therefore: an objective world of achievements, deeds, and values (this is Sisyphus's work) or the subjective world of the soul and the personality. The either–or of the living personality is concrete, individual, unique, and absolute (Jaspers, 1957).

The important thought here is that self-realization and happiness are open to everyone—not just to a chosen few—and even in the most humble and absurd situations which lack all possible hope. And this self-realization of the personality is related to an active involvement with the outside world, not just to meditating on the nature of man. Support for this thought comes from Erich Fromm, one of the major contemporary representatives of the psychoanalytic movement. In *The Fear of Freedom* he criticizes Freud for considering man a closed entity endowed with only biologically conditioned tendencies, for considering them fundamentally evil, and for interpreting the development of man's character only as a reaction to the gratification or the frustrations of these tendencies. Fromm points out that we should see the human personality through the comprehension of man's relationship with other people, with the world, with nature, and with oneself. Man is, above all, a social being and not, as Freud supposed, self-sufficient and only secondarily obliged to maintain relations with others to satisfy his instinctive needs.

According to Fromm, in *Man for Himself*, happiness is an achievement brought about by man's inner productiveness, not the satisfaction of a need springing from a physiological or psychological lack; it is the accompaniment of all productive activity in thought, feeling, and action. Productiveness is a person's ability to use his/her powers to realize the potentials inherent in him/her. To do this, man must be free and guided by reason, he must experience himself as the embodiment of his powers. In this interpretation of "productiveness" Fromm is joined by Erikson (1963), who, however, wanted to renew and improve on Freud rather than criticize him. According to both authors, productiveness is a fundamental tendency of man as a social being.

With these last authors we enter the realm of modern psychology. The terminology used may be different, but the fact remains that self-realization is described as a fundamental motivational power also in the modern systems of philosophically tinted psychological thought. "The ultimate aim and strongest desire of all mankind is to develop that fullness of life which is called personality," says Carl Jung in *The Development of Personality*. He explains that personality is the optimum development of the whole individual human being. It is the most successful adaptation to the universal conditions of existence, coupled with the greatest freedom for self-determination. Personality, as the complete realization of our whole being, is an unattainable ideal. The endeavor to attain it is a favor that is dearly paid for with conscious and unavoidable segregation. Personality cannot be developed unless the individual chooses his own way. The greatness of personalities is in their deliverance from convention, not in submission to it. Creative life always stays outside convention.

"Sutor, ne supra crepidam!" [Shoemaker, stick to your last] is a proverb that has entered other languages. A psychologist should stick with psychology and not try to set laws for the world. Jung, a great psychologist, becomes the legendary cobbler when he leads us directly into the welcoming arms of Mussolini and Hitler, the strong leaders, who assented to the power of the inner voice, and so on. However, some of the psychological ideas mentioned are remarkable. Self-realization does carry the connotation of deliverance from convention, but in this form it is an unattainable ideal, and the endeavor to accomplish it must be paid for dearly. These are the facts of life, and we build on them when outlining a solution of the problem in Chapters 2 to 4, without the inner voices. And we shall stress also the universality in the tendency to self-realization, and not restrict it to Jung's "chosen few."

This universality is anchored in our nature, holds Kurt Goldstein in his organistic approach to the problems of motivation (Goldstein, 1971). The organism reacts with general disorder and anxiety, the "catastrophic condition," to situations that hinder the realization of its capacities. The basic trend of the organism is to realize its capacities, its personality, as much as possible. Human motivation cannot be reduced to a number of isolated factors, capacities, drives. The same trend appears even in the pathological condition. Then, too, the organism tries to realize its capacities in the best possible way still within its reach.

As scientists and philosophers, Goldstein and Jung make the transition to modern psychological thought based on experimental studies. Here, too, the problems of self-realization are given prominence in various studies concerned with the motivational aspects of personality, but the continuity of human thought is neglected. The result appears in the limited character of the answers. If generalized, they are incorrect and unfair.

It is the task of this book to give a comprehensive outlook on the problems of self-realization in the "here and now" and to try to outline a theory offering answers to the multiple problems involved in this matter of prominent social, psychological, and moral importance.

REFERENCES

Alderfer, C. P. 1969. An empirical test of a new theory of human needs. *Organizational Behavior and Human Performance*, 4, 142–175.

Cajal, S. R. 1923. *Reglas y consejos sobre investigación científica*, 6th ed. Barcelona.

Camus, A. 1942. *Le mythe de Sisyphe*. Paris:Gallimard.

Erikson, E. H. 1963. *Childhood and society*, 2nd ed. New York: Norton.

Fromm, E. 1947. *Man for Himself*. New York: Rinehart,.

Fromm, E. 1971. *The Fear of Freedom*. London: Routledge.

Fromm, E. 1972. Philosophische Anthropologie und Psychanalyse. In *Philosophische Anthropologie heute*. München: C. H. Beck.

Goldstein, K. 1971. *Selected Papers*. The Hague: Martinus Nijhoff.

Heidegger, M. 1957. *Sein und Zeit*, 8th ed. Tübingen: M. Niemeyer.

Jaspers, K. 1960. *Psychologie der Weltanschauungen*. Berlin, Göttingen: Springer.

Jung, C. 1954. *The Development of Personality*. London: Routledge and Kegan Paul.

Marcel, G. 1963. *Homo Viator*. Paris: Aubier-Montaigne.

Marx, K., and Engels, F. 1970. *Die deutsche Ideologie*, Part I. Leipzig: Reclam.

Maslow, A. H. 1954. *Motivation and Personality*. New York: Harper.

Sartre, J. P. 1946. *L'existentialisme est un humanisme*. Paris: Nagel.

2

From Success to Self-Realization

Pierre L. G. Goguelin

The nineteenth century and the beginning of the twentieth were characterized by the incomplete satisfaction of primary needs—physical in the hierarchy of Maslow (1954), vital in that of Herzberg (1959), physiological in that of Hughes (1965). This led to a social tension centered on "more pay" in each occupation and on a drift of the work force toward the better paid occupations. This period is characterized by the search for a "plus," and we will call it the quantitative era (Goguelin, 1987). During this same period, as the pressure on salaries tended to diminish following increased satisfaction of vital needs, we saw a demand for security (which still belonged to the quantitative era) appear and grow. But, thanks to the increase in security measures,[1] the reduced weight of risk led simultaneously to an improvement of work conditions. Likewise, the reduced working day and working week, together with the battle against arduous tasks, while contributing to a better life by a reduction in fatigue, also resulted in increased free time for family life and the cultural development of the person through reading and audiovisual means. Thus the quantitative demands for survival moved progressively to a demand for a better life style.

The quantitative demands came exclusively from the social struggle; the possibility of a better quality of life, which was the consequence, meant much more—a better organization of that life and its realization by the individual, who ceased to be a simple reaction agent in the environment and wanted to be a positive participant in that milieu.

The authoritarian family and its social relationships corresponded to the quantitative period. The family, the father, the company, the society, decided for the young and for the man: he could only submit or rebel. The appearance of more democratic, more participative procedures, in society as well as in the company, the emergence of a dialogue between parents and children, the acknowledgment that it was rash to say to one's child "you will do as you're told until you're of age, and then you can do as you wish," the acceptance that it is preferable to prepare the young for this coming of age by making them participate in family decisions, by progressively delegating responsibility and autonomy, all this gave the young adult the capacity to take his fate in his own hands.

Along with this evolution, work—which was considered divine punishment and a sacred value—became the economic means of acquiring free time to reflect, time for oneself. Finally, habits were transformed. Cash purchases were replaced by credit, daily expenses by saving for bigger future purchases: man ceased to live on a day-to-day basis and, freed from the burden of everyday life, became accustomed to foreseeing, or, rather, learned to formulate projects.

Planning projects represents a greater evolution than foreseeing. To foresee implies a certain level of certitude—that is, that in linking with the past, a generally highly probable future can be identified for events that do not depend on us (e.g. the next eclipse of the moon). To plan a project implies futurology, a will, a zone of freedom, performing acts with a chance of success which depends on us.

Modern people are better informed; they are used to thinking about the future (they are prospective); they have a motivation (a will)—that of improving their quality of life (and, incidentally, its quantity); they enjoy a zone of freedom sufficient to reflect (free time) and to act (autonomy). Thus they meet the conditions whereby they may think on their life and, in particular, their vocational life, in project terms.

PROJECT FINALITY: SUCCESS OR SELF-REALIZATION

The problem of project finality has already been implicitly raised above, in relation to the subject of motivation: is it a motivation of the quantitative type ("wanting more") or a real qualitative motivation ("wanting better")? The former leads to the concept of success (financial and social),[2] the latter to the concept of self-realization.[3]

Success[4] is, initially, the fact of achieving a result, good or bad, to extricate oneself more or less well from a situation. In both French and English, the meaning of success and result has evolved toward a happy ending, a *good* result, as opposed to "failure." Thus, one succeeds in *something*: success is the happy solution to *one* difficulty, *one* problem, most often of external origin. Success is most often judged by social criteria: a child from a low social class who enters an engineering school and *ends* his career as Chairman and Managing Director of the company he founded has *succeeded*. However, people who have thus succeeded often commit suicide, leaving the message: "I wasted my life." How many people, having had professional and social success, say when they retire, "That was not what I wanted to do, now at last, I'll be able to do . . ." even though, from a day-to-day point of view, it is possible that they had been satisfied? A French study (Pacaud and Lahalle, 1962) showed that 66 percent of retired people, considering *only* the question of choice of work, had not been able to do what they would have liked, and *that* for fifty percent of their adult waking lives. It is therefore neither a false nor a minor problem.

To achieve, that is, to make exist as a concrete reality what only existed in the mind, is to pass from ideal to reality. "To realize oneself" is therefore to make real, to give concrete existence to a representation that we have conceived as our ideal for life, to a project. This makes us wonder: what situation would lead people to be able to say that they have fully realized themselves? In our opinion, people have realized themselves when, considering their present and their past, they are satisfied with what they have achieved and what they have become, that they would do the same again, that they feel at peace with themselves, and that they will continue without regret to organize their development in the same perspective. Let us at this point emphasize "development," because the future can only be "what will happen to them," whereas their development contains "what they will make of themselves" in the possible future.

Success is therefore linked to a narrow sphere, to a particular problem, whereas the realization, "what we want to make of ourselves, by ourselves, and in ourselves," is global: we have fully realized ourselves. Therefore there can be success without self-realization, and the sum of all the hoped for successes does not necessarily bring about self-realization: it can favour it, but the realization operates at another level. Similarly, there can be realization without success because success means achievement, a way out of difficulty, whereas realization is a development and a permanent quest: we do not say that a saint succeeded because his name is on the calendar, just as other great men have their names in "Who's Who" or in the dictionary; however, he has certainly realized himself, even if he died as a martyr, in surpassing himself.

In all that follows, we will give preference to the self-realization finality, success only indicating the happy resolution of a cognitive-economico-social problem. In so doing we will remain faithful to the historical evolution of our societies, from the quantity to the quality of life.

THE CONCEPT OF SELF-REALIZATION

Does a Sign Indicating Self-Realization Exist?

The sign of personal realization is not wisdom, which is so often the camouflage of resignation, of renunciation, even pusilanimity ("after all, it was not that bad," "the wise man is satisfied with little," "you must be philosophical in life," etc.). In reality, we have not found any word describing the overall behavior (in the sense of "observable responses") of people who have realized themselves. The concept of serenity could perhaps be the nearest, but serene people can simply be wise as described above; on the other hand, if one can be tormented on the way to realization, it seems to me that the final state, when it is realized and then goes on, is serenity.

This leads to another observation: ultimately, there is no observable sign of the state of self-realization. It is an inner state proper to the person who is trying to achieve his own realization or who had already realized himself: it can therefore only be recognized by him and can only be revealed to us by what he can tell us about it. It seems to us that what can best express it is the state of nonregret: "if it were to be redone, I would do the same again," which indicates the agreement between what we hope for most deeply and what we have become.

The Factors of Self-Realization, the Diversity of Origins

Self-realization is thus a highly personal problem, which implies a great variety of "self-realization." We must therefore ask ourselves about the channels of approach that make it possible to identify the factors necessary to establish such self-realization.

A first line of approach could be psychoanalysis: to realize oneself is to become what I would hope to be, that is, become consistent with my ideal ego. The problem is then that of confrontation of the channels used to attain it with the imperatives of my superego, or again the confrontation of the ideal ego with the ideal of the ego. An unresolved or unsolvable conflict will prevent any possibility of self-realization, with several eventualities: permanent conflict, which creates a tortured individual; the triumph of one or two dimensions over the other, which can create either the individual who thinks he is entrusted with a mission and transcends the conflict through sacrifice, or the voluntarist. The latter either crushes the others through success in a certain area, in a sphere, or becomes completely boxed in. For this latter, we should perhaps talk of pathological self-realization, as is passion in relation to interest.

A second line of approach, more experimental and social, would be to speak in terms of level of aspiration, needs, aims and objectives, interests, inclinations, trends, even attitudes, values, incorporating all this under the general term of motivation. But, allowing for changes with age, our ideal of life should stabilize with maturity, otherwise we run the risk of dispersing our talents. So motivation is most often taken in the sense of what will determine our actions in the context of an environment which, by nature, is variable. At this point, motivation can be directed exclusively by an inner and personal factor, which would guide us in a permanent way almost all our life. One particular extreme case would be that of a vocational calling where the individual knows, sometimes while still very young, what he wants to do and "sacrifices" everything to attain his objectives. We have intentionally put sacrifice in inverted commas, because was it really a sacrifice for him? On the contrary, would it not have been a sacrifice for him (*plus feelings of guilt*) had he had to renounce his vocation, so as not to displease his family, for instance.

Let us note that the problem of vocational calling is mysterious; it often appears very early in life and manifests itself as an uncontrollable force "which pushes," but an explanation for which can be found neither in the individual nor in his background. Can we imagine there being something innate, something that would "express itself" in the individual, in the same way as we now recognize a genetic predisposition to specific organic and psychic troubles?

According to a third line of approach, we could therefore place ourselves at the level of what "unconsciously pushes us." Psychologists—even non-psychoanalysts, ethologists, behavioral biologists—under various designations (e.g. aggressive drives or system-regulating aggression, etc.) generally acknowledge five or six types of drives: physical self-preservation; pleasure or sexual drives; aggression (with defence of territory); gregarious drives (which introduce the weight of others and society); ego-defence and self-assertive drive; even those of attachment (Goguelin, 1972).

If we take a closer look, in everyday language we find the terms to love, to have, to be able, to be. Any one of these forces can be stronger than the others, merge with them, and control them in the sense of the individual architectonics of G. A. Kelly (1955) and J. R. Adams Webber (1979). Thus, we come to understand people who center their personal realization on power, on knowledge (another form of power), on money for itself and as a means to an end, on the predominance of emotional life, and so forth. We have to notice that, here again, the finalities are numerous, often conflicting, and, in the case where one of them would smother all the others, we would probably revert to the notions of success and failure.

The first conclusion can be drawn: the factors that can lead to self-realization are numerous, they differ from one individual to another, and they are highly personal: it is *the problem of each individual.*

The Reference Element of Self-Realization, the Diversity of Cases

To realize oneself implies becoming faithful to a certain model—which can be concrete (i.e. a man, a woman who exists or has existed) or abstract (i.e. without reference to a known person)—that composes the ideal person that we would hope to become.

This being, whether concrete or abstract, constitutes the reference element of self-realization: if we draw close enough to it, at the very least if we draw close enough to the representation of what we make of it, we realize ourselves. In certain cases, the demand will be higher and we will try to surpass it.

Let us take the simplest case, where the model is an existing person, endowed with all the qualities which are projected on him or her by the subject. Many boys and girls take as a model an actor or actress, a singer or a sporting personality. They go so far as to imitate the voice, the bearing, the hair-style, even dressing the same way. For the subject, the ever-present question is: "if my model were in my place, what would s/he do?" This may go as far as being totally blind to oneself, to one's own physical appearance, mental capacities, and so forth. Here, we are confronted with a sort of pathology of self-realization by identification with a model, and, we might even say, with a hero. Without going so far, a good number of our contemporaries have, deep down, a secret admiration for characters whom they try to bring to life in themselves.

The most complex case is one where the reference element has been constructed by the individual either from several characters, or directly from what s/he is (see above, the lines of approach), but this supposes a vast knowledge of oneself. The reference element is more likely to appear progressively from the interaction between what we are (and what we partially ignore being) and the characters who strike a sympathetic chord with what we are and who play, in some way, the role of revealer. We can thus formulate the reference element without always being conscious of what we are seeking in the realization of ourselves.

However, this does not exclude the influence of the environment on the formation of the reference element:

1. The reference can operate independently of the milieu (or in opposition to it). A robot, programmed (finalized) permanently and acting according to this program, achieves its ends; we cannot say that it realizes itself since it is not endowed with reflection and free will, but we can keep the image. Certain people realize themselves through simple reference to what they believe to be ideal, independently of what others may think: "Only you count". This can be judged, by society, either as an extraordinary, astonishing success, or as the sign of fundamental inadaptation—"he's a failure"—but the person himself feels misunderstood and lives by the idea that he is right, regardless of all the others. Sometimes, the next generation recognizes such a person as a genius. We are here talking about people who are egocentric, independent, and rather antisocial.

2. The reference can be: "oneself for and by the image reflected by others" in the sense of "social other" (the family, activity groups, etc.); the most important thing is to become accepted, to become true to the personality approved by these groups. In training, in group work, and particularly in psychodramas, we know how numerous the participants are who discover a social image of themselves totally different from what they had imagined. We know the impact that

the awareness reflected through others has on the individual. Some reconsider themselves and, on the surface, present a "different face," appearing to conform more to what is expected of them (which also means that they do not resolve their inner conflict but start playing a role). Others change deeply, remodelling themselves to attain another being, that is, another level of inner coherence. The former can only realize themselves in agreement with society, and only this agreement can give them a feeling (apparent) of fulfillment, of culmination: they are dependent. The latter use the reflected image to be better accepted while maintaining their autonomy.

3. The reference can be: "oneself in confrontation with society and a world of which we feel we form an integral part (alienation) and toward which we have certain duties." There is no possible self-realization until we have managed to transform this society, this world, according to our idea—we have a mission to accomplish: politicians, ideologists, trade unionists, even, for example, ecologists, fall into this category.

4. The reference can be: "oneself facing the Universe, the celestial powers, God." Self-realization can either take effect within oneself, with more or less withdrawal in relation to the external world (a borderline case being, for example, a religious recluse), or forcefully introducing yourself into the world (e.g. a church missionary).

The second conclusion can be drawn: the reference element of self-realization differs from one individual to another and is also highly personal.

The Ways of Self-Realization, the Diversity of Cases

Finally let us consider the possible ways of self-realization, which, let us not forget, is essentially qualitative. These ways can become spheres of success if they are followed separately in a quantitative perspective only, that of completing a performance.

Some seek their realization through the body: physical harmony, care of the body, and so forth. Success is illustrated by muscular development (Mr. Muscles, body building, etc.) or surpassing oneself in performance (jogging, competitive sport, etc.).

Some center on the development of their mental capacities, seeking to organize their knowledge, to be rational, whereas others seek the quantitative, to be intellectual through the development of their memory, through intellectual training or the development of the will: there are fast-reading champions and degree collectors.

Some concentrate on understanding the world and building a culture, whereas others aim at the accumulation of knowledge, often in an advanced field, becoming the undisputed specialist.

Some concentrate on creation, which is the synthesis of knowledge and know-how, while others are known for knowing or knowing how to do many isolated things. Finally, some concentrate on knowing how to appear, which leads to a form of social success.

This list is certainly not complete, but it does clearly show us the difference between self-realization and success and how one passes "easily" from one to the other when quantity takes precedence over quality.

If we look around us, we see that each one of us adheres to a restricted number of these ways of self-realization. This leads us to the third conclusion: self-realization can be achieved through very different channels, one of which often prevails.

CONCLUSION

If it is possible to define a mark indicating self-realization, the factors—the origins—are multiple; it is the same for reference elements and ways of achieving them. Self-realization is therefore a highly personal problem: we must, as individuals, try to see ourselves clearly, to become aware of our reference element or elements (a person, ourselves, others, society, the Universe) and the way or ways in which or through which we will achieve our own personal realization; the diversities of these ways, and consequently their specificity to the person, is as great as that of fingerprints.

It is clear that to impose on a third party our reference elements and ways of self-realization would be meaningless because the factors pushing us, motivating us, are surely very different from anyone else's. This does not mean, however, that each one of us must be abandoned to him/herself? It is possible to obtain help to make progress in elucidating the problem. The Vocational Project and the Planning of Training, discussed in Chapter 9, are part of this help.

NOTES

1. In France: 1898: coverage for accidents at work; 1910: pensions for manual and agricultural workers; 1930: national insurance; 1932: family allowance; 1945: the creation of the National Health Service; 1958: unemployment benefit. At present, "the state retracing the social effort of the Nation," or social budget, covers the various allowances from which families benefit: illness, invalidity, old age, death, maternity, family situation, housing, accidents at work, professional illness, and various disasters.

2. Success corresponds to the need for social connections, for esteem (Maslow, 1954) and to the need for recognition, responsibility, and esteem (Hughes, 1965).

3. Self-realization corresponds to the need for accomplishment (A. H. Maslow and C. L. Hughes).

4. From Latin *uscita*; cf. issue, in French, and, in English, to succeed: from Latin *succedere*; succès in French, success in English—whatever, good or bad, occurs following an act.

REFERENCES

Goguelin, P. 1972. *Psychologie générale*, Paris: Centre de Documentation Universitaire.

Goguelin, P. 1987. Vers une nouvelle psychologie du travail. *Revue de Psychologie Appliquée* 37(2): 139–174.

Herzberg, F. 1959. *Motivation at Work*. New York: John Wiley.

Kelly, G. A. 1955. *The Psychology of Personal Construct*. New York: Norton.

Maslow, A. H. 1954. *Motivation and Personality*. New York: Harper.

Pacaud, S., and Lahalle, M. 1962. Quelques données sur les attitudes dans la vieillesse à l'égard de la profession qui fut exercée au cours de la vie et à l'égard de la professon rêvée dans la jeunesse. *Hygiène mentale*, 1: 25–40.

Webber, J. R. Adams. 1979. *Personal Construct Theory, Concepts and Applications*. New York: John Wiley.

3

Money and Self-Realization: New Trends in Western Culture

Abraham K. Korman

Income level has long been considered to be of major significance in Western cultures as a factor influencing the process of self-realization. Intrinsic to these cultures are such beliefs as the expectation that money will provide the means by which one can more fully satisfy one's personal desires and needs. In addition, high income has also been viewed as providing the means by which one can more fully satisfy the needs of one's family and thus, by enabling the increased satisfaction of one's affiliative needs, increase a sense of self-realization even further.

In this chapter we will undertake an examination of recent research relevant to these traditional views on the significance of money and higher levels of income for the self-realization process in Western cultures. We shall see that the findings that are available suggest that the significance of money for self-realization is not quite in keeping with these traditional expectations. Furthermore, there is also an indication that the significance of money and income may well be changing in Western societies and that new questions are beginning to be raised concerning the role of income in facilitating the attainment of self-realization. Thus, it will be shown that several paradoxes have developed in Western cultures concerning the meaning of money and high income levels. One paradox is that while there is a continuing belief in the value of materialism for the attainment of self-realization, with a loss of feelings of the latter when such values from income are not realized (cf. Korman, Mahler, and Omran, 1983), there is apparently little value for money in its symbolic form and the promises it may hold for self-realization.

In addition, there is also an increasing belief that there is an inherent conflict between the attainment of both career success (including financial rewards) and affiliative satisfactions, and that both cannot be attained if each is sought to a maximal extent. Further adding to the increasingly perceived ambiguity as to the role of money in impacting on self-realization is the evidence suggesting that males appear to view money as a source of power and, thus, of potential self-realization; the same sense of power may, however, serve to alienate one from others and thus act as a source of difficulty in reaching a sense of self-realization through the aid of others. The still meager evidence that is available suggests that women, on the other hand, do not view power and money and their interrelationships in the same manner as do men.

For these reasons it may be argued that the significance of income for implementing self-realization in contemporary Western societies may be undergoing signficant changes as a result of these paradoxical patterns whose resolving is not immediately apparent. Furthermore, the directions in which such changes are occurring are also unclear at this time, partially because traditional views of money and the importance of the benefits it may provide also remain strong. As a result, it is difficult at this time to make clear predictions as to what the significance of income for self-realization will be in the future.

In the following we will develop these arguments in greater detail and make more explicit the rationale for the conclusions we have suggested. In undertaking this analysis we will limit our consideration to those instances where one's income level has resulted from personally and/or family-earned income. Similarly, we will define a high degree of self-realization as being descriptive of those individuals whose interactions with the world are reflective of one's "real, full" self, as self-perceived. Those idividuals who interact in the world every day with other people and things, but who perceive that that person (or "self") who is doing the interacting is not his/her "real, full self" but rather some superficial portion of that self, will be defined as personally alienated (or the converse of "self-realized"). For the latter individuals, the "real self" is hidden underneath, does not see the light of day, and is different from, separate from, and estranged from the "expressed self"—the "self" that does interact with the world every day. For the self-realized self, the self that does interact is the real self.

It may be noted that this view of the self-realization process as essentially the converse of personal alienation is in line with the conceptualization of these constructs by Weiss (1962) who saw alienation as being, in its most active form, the rejection of being oneself and the attempt to become some other, more ideal self. Alienation, in his view, is not the process of self-realization but rather an escape from the hated self into some ideal self. It is, to paraphrase terms used by Karen Horney, a remoteness from one's own feelings, wishes, beliefs, and energies and from the active, spontaneous core of oneself.

RESEARCH FINDINGS:
THE SYMBOLIC VALUE OF MONEY
AS AN IMPACT ON SELF-REALIZATION

Theories have long been proposed that money and income can be viewed as "generalized conditioned reinforcers" or as "symbolic anxiety reducers" in order to explain their continued and, in some cases, apparently addictive attractiveness to those who appear to have little concrete need for higher levels of income (cf. Brown, 1961; Slater, 1980). In the "generalized conditioned reinforcer" perspective money is proposed as attaining its symbolic significance as a source of positive value because of its continued pairing with primary reinforcers, whereas in the "generalized anxiety-reducer" view it is argued that a major function of income is to reduce the negative feelings one may have in the absence of money. In addition, money may also have great symbolic value because the sense of power it is reputed to provide may enable one to ignore the anxiety that one may feel from possible disapproving others when expressing a desire to realize one's personal values and beliefs either in the present or in the future.

Despite the intuitive appeal of these arguments, the research evidence that has accumulated during the past several decades suggests that such symbolic value of income may have been vastly overstated and that we need to look elsewhere to explain the appeal of income to many individuals. In brief, there has been little evidence to support such a hypothesis, either in research reported more than two decades ago (Opsahl and Dunnette, 1966) or in a review of more recent vintage which summarized nineteen studies in the literature relating to the relationship between income and well-being (Korman, Omran, and Mahler, 1983). In most of the studies cited in the latter review the measure of well-being used was life- and/or marital satisfaction, but in three cases actual measures of self-realization (as defined above) were utilized (Maddi, Kobasa, and Hoover, 1981; Vredenburgh and Sheridan, 1979; Korman, Omran, and Mahler, 1983). Regardless of the measure of well-being used, there were few relationships of any significance. In ten of the studies there were no significant correlations at all, while in the others most of the correlations were insignificant or rather trivial in value, even if statistically significant. These conclusions held true as much for the studies where a specific measure self-realization was employed as for those where other measures of well-being were employed. In the Maddi study only three of eighteen correlations were significant, whereas in the Korman et al. research the comparable figures were two of twenty-eight correlations reaching statistical significance. In the latter case, the samples were subgrouped and combined in different ways to tease out possible relationships even in an exploratory manner, but the effort was generally unsuccessful. Also unsuccessful in an effort to identify any systematic relationship was the Vredenburgh and Sheridan study, where the results were either insignificant or inconsistent, with no discernible pattern.

In essence, the data in these studies suggest little or no relationship between income and feelings of well-being, despite the oft-professed symbolic value of money and its promise of material satisfactions, whether such well-being is measured by life satisfaction, marital satisfaction, or feelings of self-realization.

RESEARCH FINDINGS:
THE SIGNIFICANCE OF MATERIALISTIC
SATISFACTIONS FOR FEELINGS
OF SELF-REALIZATION

Although there appears to be little support for the importance of income level as a conditioned reinforcer or as a symbolic anxiety reducer which provides promise of future self-realization, there is support for the hypothesis that the material values that are obtainable with higher income levels are important for the process of self-realization. In brief, as Vroom (1964) and others have proposed, when money and income are seen as having instrumental value for the achievement of concrete outcomes, the results are greater feelings of self-realization. On the other hand, if these outcomes are not obtained, then the results are in the opposite direction.

Among the studies conducted in the United States which support this conclusion are those by Crocitto (1986), in her research with physicians and dentists, and the series of studies by Korman and his coworkers (Korman, Wittig-Berman, and Lang, 1981; Korman et al., in preparation). The basic framework used in these latter studies was to relate the extent to which higher levels of income had actually led to better materialistic outcomes to the Personal Alienation subscale of the Philosophy of Life measure (Korman, Wittig-Berman, and Lang, 1981). The latter is a Likert-type questionnaire which continues to undergo and to be supported by various construct validation analyses as a useful measure of personal alienation (cf. Korman et al., in preparation). In these cases personal alienation has been defined as opposite to that of self-realization and, consistent with the definition offered above, as the cognition that one's everyday behavior reflects some surface, superficial aspect of the self and does not reflect a "real self" which is being impoverished as a result of its lack of exposure to the everyday world. In general, the results of these studies are consistent, indicating clearly that the more that money is viewed as incapable of generating a higher level of concrete consumer goods and satisfactions, the higher the level of personal alienation (and the lower the level of self-realization). Also of interest in

Table 3.1
Relationships between Disconfirmed Value of Income and Lack of
Self-Realization

Sample Type	r	Sig. level	N
School of business alumni sample[1]	59	0.01	82
M.B.A. Sample[1]	53	0.01	67
1981 Sample—managers and professionals[2]	23	0.01	173
1983 Sample—managers and professionals[2]	20	0.01	110
College students[2]	33	0.01	100
Northern Italian[3]	49	0.01	102
Southern Italian[3]	60	0.01	88

Sources:

[1]A. K. Korman, U. Wittig-Berman, and D. Lang, 1981. Career Success and Personal Failure: Alienation in Professionals and Managers. *Academy of Management Journal,* 24(2): 342–360.

[2]A. K. Korman, J. Greenberg, D. Lang, S. Mahler, C. Lavy, and K. Omran, *A Study of the Relationships between Income Level and Alienation.* Baruch College, 1987. Paper to be submitted for publication.

[3]R. Bellu, A. K. Korman, C. Lavy, and J. Greenberg, 1987. *A Cross-Cultural Study of Personal and Social Alienation.* Baruch College: Paper to be submitted for publication.

these studies is that similar findings were obtained when college-age students from varying economic backgrounds were assessed by similar measures. In these studies also, the more that money was perceived as generating outcomes such as poor consumer products, poor services, and so forth, the lower the degree of self-realization reported by the college-student respondents. There is also evidence that this generalization concerning the significance of material satisfactions as an impact on self-realization is not limited to the U.S. setting but also occurs in other Western societies. This has been shown in a careful test of this hypothesis in northern and southern Italy (Bellu, Korman, Lavy, and Greenberg, mimeo). Utilizing forward and back translation procedures through three iterations in order to develop accurate Italian language versions of the original measures used in the United States, Bellu and his coworkers found even stronger relationships than those found for the U.S. samples. Table 3.1 provides a summary of Bellu's findings, together with those from the several studies reported by Korman and his co-investigators.

Explanations for the continuing viability of materialistic satisfactions as providing significant impact on feelings of self-realization may reflect both cultural and psychological factors. One explanation for the high value placed on money in the U.S. culture rests in the hypothesis that there are few other bonds to tie the United States together as a nation and as a people, particularly in view of the cataclysmic societal changes that have occurred during the past two decades. The legally required separation of church and state precludes religious bonds of commonality in the United States (despite recent efforts to change such division), and the ties that bound the nation together during such times of stress as World War II appear to have long since dissipated, if indeed they were ever as strong as U.S. mythology suggests. Consistent also with this view of the unifying influence of a high value for money and the materialistic satisfactions it leads to is its possible influence as a factor underlying the migrations so deeply ingrained in U.S. history. The movement of millions from Europe to the New World and from the East Coast to the West had multiple motives, as all such mass migrations generally do, but the desire for a more materially satisfying life style was clearly involved. It is also reasonable to assume that such motivational factors were also involved in the migrations of black Americans from the South to the North during the post–World-War-II period and, more recently, the migrations to the United States from the nations of the Pacific. Such values underlying both the original and more recent migrations have led to what Slater (1970) has termed our value for "linear theories of progress," that is, the view that human progress and human satisfactions depend on "money and power" and the outcomes they can bring. Thus, it may be that a value for money and materialism, and the view that it is through such values that self-realization may be attained, may be so ingrained in U.S. cultural values and socialization patterns that any attempt to decrease their significance may run up against strong psychological and social barriers.

Yet, despite the possible viability of these explanations for the U.S. setting, it would appear, at least at first glance, that their usefulness for the Italian setting, north or south, may not be as great. Italy, despite its history, is a far more homogenous culture than the United States and has been marked by far greater bonds of commonality of family life and religion than has been typically true in the U.S. setting. On the other hand, it needs also to be pointed out that the traditional bonds of Italian life have become quite loosened in recent years with such changes as the separation of the government from its official ties with the Church, the continued strength of the political parties of the left, and the acceptance of such traditionally controversial changes as divorce and abortion rights. Perhaps the recency of these changes and their significance in a society with the traditions of Italian culture have made material satisfaction as important (or even more, considering the size of the correlations in Table 3.1) than in the long-established "free" U.S. setting.

Whatever the explanation for these findings in the U.S. and/or Italian settings, and it is clear that much research is needed on these issues, it appears reasonable to conclude that, despite the growth of theories of self-actualization and similar psychological constructs during the past two decades, the role of income level and the importance of the concrete material satisfactions it is expected to provide continues to remain of great significance in Western nations for understanding the attainment of self-realization. While such goals as self-implementation in one's career as a factor affecting feelings of over-all self-realization have gained increasing visibility and may in fact be crucially important under some conditions, research results continue to point to the continued significance of income levels as mechanisms for the attainment of material goods as one key to the understanding of the self-realization process. In essence, when the increased consumer satisfactions thought to be consistent with higher income occur and when other perceived correlates of higher income actually take place (e.g. more interesting jobs), feelings of self-realization are high. On the other hand, when these effects and/or correlates do not occur and income level is thereby rendered meaningless as a cue to increased consumer satisfactions and related benefits, then self-realization is lower.

THE ACHIEVEMENT/AFFILIATION CONFLICT: THE GROWTH OF NORMLESSNESS AND ITS IMPLICATIONS FOR SELF-REALIZATION

Achievement and affiliative needs have long been considered to be key, if not the key, human needs. Much of society and its structures are built around mechanisms designed to facilitate satisfactions in these areas, and until the mid-1960s U.S. culture was reasonably coherent in the norms it set as to how one met one's achievement and affiliative needs. In general, the male was directly responsible for the attainment of achievement satisfactions, while the female satisfied her particular needs in these areas indirectly through the cooperation of the male. Similarly, the female was directly responsible for the attainment of affiliative satisfactions, and the male attained his satisfactions in this area indirectly through the cooperation of the female. In addition, higher levels of career success and the higher levels of income that went along with such success were assumed to facilitate both processes (Korman, Mahler, and Omran, 1983).

In recent years it has seemed apparent that these norms have broken down for a significant segment of our society with alternative guides to behavior not as yet readily available. The implications of career success and its financial rewards for familial and other affiliative satisfactions have become increasingly questionable and are seen in many cases as having either negative or at best problematic implications (Korman and Korman, 1980; Korman, in press). In brief, for many of those who seek and attain higher levels of income, the development and maintenance of friendships and family life have become increasingly difficult. Some recent indication of

Table 3.2
Perceptions of Interactive Problems of Work Careers and Family Life

	% Agreeing	
	Men	*Women*
Say that job interferes with family life	37.2	40.9
Refused a job, promotion, or transfer because it would mean less family life.	29.6	25.7
Sought less demanding job to get more family time.	20.5	26.5
Think children of working parents suffer by not being given enough time and attention	55.4	58.2

Source: F. S. Chapman, "Executive Guilt: Who's Taking Care of the Children?" *Fortune*, April 14, 1987: 35.

the extent to which questions and problems have arisen in our society as to the mechanisms by which both sources of satisfaction may be attained is shown in a survey of 400 working couples reported in *Fortune* (Chapman, 1987). Table 3.2 reports some of the findings relevant to this question.

Increasingly, normative guidelines as to how one can attain the satisfaction of both achievement and affiliative desires do not seem to be readily apparent for significant numbers of American men and women, and, to the extent that an individual perceives and is affected by such normlessness, the result is often a decline in feelings of self-realization. In the research cited earlier by Korman and his associates and by the research team in Italy, the results show clearly that personal alienation (i.e. a lack of self-realization in one's life) is significantly greater among those who see difficulties in attaining affiliative satisfactions while also attempting to achieve career and financial success. The findings are clear and consistent both in the United States and in Italy, as Table 3.3 indicates.

Also of importance for our concerns here is the fact that the impact of this type of perceived normlessness on feelings of self-realization (or the lack of same) appears to affect both men and women in the American samples. (Such breakdowns were not available for the Italian samples.) Evidence for the effect of such normlessness on both sexes is presented in Table 3.4.

Unanswered, however, by these findings is the question as to whether the processes involved are similar for both genders. The tangential evidence that is available suggests that they may not be. Thus, there is some indication that, for males, the realization of the inability to attain both achievement and affiliative satisfactions may come only after the achievement effort has taken place and the expected affiliative satisfactions have not occurred (cf. Evans and Bartoleme, 1981). One reason for these patterns may be the type of assumptions made by males at the time of setting out on a career. Grief and Munter (1980) have described such original career assumptions on the part of men as follows:

1. As the male moves forward in his career, his family will either remain static or develop according to his wishes and expectations;
2. The male will eventually be able to limit and modify voluntarily, at will, a career pattern established over the years during which the family accepted second place in his life;
3. The male will be able to pick up where he left off in terms of his family life, as though the years of deprivation during which his career was first in his value system did not matter;
4. The rewards he will achieve during the years when his career assumed first place in his value system will be so great both to him and his family that his years of neglect will be justified;
5. The satisfactions he will receive by operating on a career-first basis will be sufficient to sustain him personally, even if familial problems do develop.

Table 3.3
Relationships between Perceived Difficulty in Attaining both Achievement and Affiliative Satisfactions and Lack of Self-Realization

Sample Type	r	Sig. level	N
School of business alumni sample[1]	57	0.01	82
M.B.A. Sample[1]	50	0.01	67
1981 Sample—managers and professionals[2]	34	0.01	173
1983 Sample—managers and professionals[2]	22	0.01	110
Northern Italian[3]	36	0.01	102
Southern Italian[3]	47	0.01	88

Sources:

[1]A. K. Korman, U. Wittig-Berman, and D. Lang, 1981. Career Success and Personal Failure: Alienation in Professionals and Managers. *Academy of Management Journal,* 24(2): 342–360.

[2]A. K. Korman, J. Greenberg, D. Lang, S. Mahler, C. Lavy, and K. Omran, 1987. *A Study of the Relationships between Income Level and Alienation.* Baruch College. Paper to be submitted for publication.

[3]R. Bellu, A. K. Korman, C. Lavy, and J. Greenberg, 1987. *A Cross-Cultural Study of Personal and Social Alienation.* Baruch College: Paper to be submitted for publication.

Table 3.4

Relationships between Sense of Normlessness Concerning the Attainment of Both Achievement and Affiliation and a Sense of Self-Realization According to Gender

Sample	r	Sig. level	N
Total	34	0.01	173
Females	23	0.05	71
Males	41	0.01	99

Source: A. K. Korman, J. Greenberg, D. Lang, S. Mahler, C. Lavy, and K. Omran, 1987. *The Achievement/Affiliation Conflict in Organizational Life and Personal/Social Alienation.* Baruch College. Paper to be submitted for publication.

Most of the evidence we have suggests that males often do not derive the positive benefits they have expected, with the possible exception of the fifth assumption. For example, Evans and Bartoleme, in the study cited above of male European managers and executives, found that while some of their career and financially successful respondents expressed considerable dissatisfaction with the way in which they had organized their lives and great unhappiness about their neglect of their families, they still did not really express a desire to change anything. On the other hand, the studies have provided evidence that while male managers may operate on the basis of the first four assumptions, their expectations are rarely ever met. A recent study of successful entrepreneurs found that nearly half said they underestimated the impact that starting a business would have on their lives and that more than half said they had dramatically reduced the time spent with their families and their leisure activities (*USA TODAY*, 1986). In addition, 36 percent said the pressure of running the business had damaged their relationship with their spouse, and 22 percent said their marital relationship was a major source of stress. There is additional evidence for the same conclusions in studies of males which show (a) a loss of psychological well-being and the growth of a sense of isolation among successful entrepreneurs (Gumpert and Boyd, 1984); (b) an increased avoidance of others and a keeping of emotions to oneself among successful managers (Maccoby, 1976); and (c) a general realization of the cost on family life among executives that has taken place as a result of career commitments and their drive toward upward success (Kofomidos, 1984). While a few of these studies included some women as part of their sample, the overwhelming majority of the individuals under study were male.

Such lack of sampling from both genders in these studies has had a beneficial effect since there is some reason to think, on the basis of independent studies, that while successful, affluent women may exhibit similar negative reaction to the increased normlessness in our society concerning mechanisms for attaining both achievement and affiliative satisfactions, the processes and patterns involved are somewhat different. One hypothesis for explaining such potential gender differences may be that women executives do not lose contact with their needs for affiliative satisfactions during their drive for success, as men may be more apt to because of the difficulties men tend to have in dealing with their interpersonal problems (Bartoleme, 1972; Bartoleme, 1983). Gilligan (1982) has provided a theoretical rationale for such gender differences as a result of differences in socialization processes. According to her, men are socialized for independence, for logical thinking, and for avoidance of intimacy and closeness with others. They therefore grow up to be autonomous (or are encouraged to be so) and to fear a close relationship with others most of all. Women, on the other hand, Gilligan argues, are socialized for dependency, for interrelationships with others, and for fear of separation. Her progress to maturity is measured as a function of the relationships she develops, and her greatest fear becomes autonomy.

Yet, it may be that it is in remaining in contact with affiliation feelings and attempting to satisfy the need both for affiliation and for achievement may lead to a lack of self-realization despite career and financial success. Evidence supporting this conclusion comes in the 1986 study reported by Korman and his coworkers cited earlier (Korman et al., 1986). In this study relationships between income level and feelings of self-realization were determined for male and female managers and professionals who had first been subgrouped on the basis of the degree to which they were experiencing a lack of affiliative satisfactions in their lives. Women were found to be significantly more willing than men to admit to an increasing lack of self-realization in their lives with increasing income levels. For women, there was a positive correlation of 0.35 (significant at 0.01 level) between income level and lack of self-realization (or personal alienation) for those who were experiencing high degrees of lack of affiliative satisfaction, whereas the comparable correlation for males was an insignificant negative relationship of 0.24 (which was also significantly different from the correlation for women).

However, it is important to keep in mind that much of the evidence we have concerning possible gender differences in this area is still in the anecdotal stage, and that systematic empirical data are lacking (cf. Deutsch, 1986). Similarly, while theoretical arguments such as those of Gilligan and others who have suggested similar processes are intuitively appealing, such appeal is not the same as evaluation by appropriate research investigations. As of this writing, such comparative gender studies have still to be conducted in the context of reactions to career and financial success.

THE AMBIGUITIES OF POWER AND POWERLESSNESS
AS FACTORS IN SELF-REALIZATION

The impact that the attainment of power has on the self-realization process appears to be rather ambiguous despite the traditional beliefs concerning the role of powerlessness in the generation of feelings of alienation. One major reason for such ambiguity is research findings showing that high levels of power may be as alienating from others as feelings of powerlessness. There is evidence in the work of Kipnis (1976) that the possession of power relative to others, particularly in hierarchical settings, may have negative, rather than positive, effects on the person who has attained the power position in terms of relationships to others. In a series of experimental and field investigations, Kipnis presented evidence showing how the attainment of hierarchical power tended to lead to a separation from others and an increasing sense of social alienation. Since such social alienation may then generate a decline of affiliative need satisfactions and a decline in the ability to ask others for help in one's self-realization process, one effect of the attainment of power might then be a decline in one's sense of self-realization. Thus, although powerlessness has long been known to have negative effects for self-realization (cf. Kornhauser, 1965), it would appear that attaining power positions may result in similar outcomes. Such contradictory findings would appear to generate unclear inferences concerning the implications of higher levels of income, often associated with power positions and a perceived benefit of power, in the self-realization process. One possibility is that there may be a U-shaped relationship between power (and money) on the one hand and, on the other, a sense of self-realization. That is, individuals with low levels of power (and income) are unable to achieve any meaningful level of self-realization because of a lack of the necessary resources to attain such an outcome. On the other hand, it may also be that those with a very high level of power (and income) may become arrogant and unrealistic in their expectations and come to believe that they deserve to attain whatever they wish as a result of their power and wealth status. Such expectations may lead to alienation from others, thus losing their aid and perhaps also generating in these other individuals a sense of hostility and antagonism. Such processes may then lead to a loss of capability to attain any sense of self-realization that depends in part on the cooperation of others. In addition, it has also been proposed that one of the impacts of high-income (and power) positions may be a loss of contact with various dimensions of personal self-needs in favor of a view of the self as essentially reflecting a financial value and little else (cf. Slater, 1970).

However, despite the intuitive appeal of some of these arguments, there is as yet little research that can provide rigorous tests of these proposals. This lack and the general difficulty of adequately testing U-shaped relationships

(Korman, 1974, Chap. 5) suggests that we are still a considerable distance from meaningful empirically supported generalizations as to the impact of money, power, and their interactions on the self-realization process.

A further complication is that there is some indication that gender differences may also contribute a further source of ambiguity in developing an understanding of the role of money, feelings of power, and feelings of self-realization. The research findings that are available suggest that money may not have the same significance for women as for men. In one study conducted by the author and his co-workers a high significant positive correlation between income and feelings of self-realization was found for males describing themselves as high in powerlessness, whereas the correlation for females with the same levels of powerlessness was insignificant and significantly lower from that of the males (Korman et al., 1986). One reason may be that higher levels of income may be viewed as an alternative source of power by men but less so by women, either in a contemporary sense or in terms of future promise. Why these different reactions to money on the part of men and women? One hypothesis is that we are a materialistic culture which has greatly valued "money and income" as a criterion for the evaluation of individuals and organizations and that it has been men who have been mostly responsible for the development and utilization of this criterion (cf. Slater, 1970). To turn their backs on this criterion is to reject, or so it would seem, a world that they have made.

SUMMARY

There are currently several contradictory patterns in American life concerning the impact of money and income on the process of self-realization. While on the one hand its possession appears to have very little symbolic value, there is support for the prediction that self-realization will decline when money becomes meaningless in the sense that it does not buy what it is supposed to buy. The meaningfulness of money as to the concrete materialistic satisfactions it may purchase, to use the terminology proposed by Seeman (1972), appears to be an important factor in the process of self-realization. Should such meaningfulness not occur—that is, the satisfactions it purchases are not appropriate to the costs and the money involved—then self-realization decreases. Also important is normlessness, or the lack of societal guidelines as to how one attains desired outcomes relative to achievement and affiliative satisfactions and how one should view the value of money. Is money a good thing to be treasured and sought, or is it to be avoided as a source of familial and affiliative disintegration? A lack of clear normative guidelines as to how to attain both types of satisfaction and the role of money and high income levels in such attainment will also generate a lower level of self-realization. Also confusing are the implications of power and powerlessness (and its correlates of high and low income) since there is some indication that both extremes may have a negative effect on feelings of self-realization.

Given these stable and also changing views on the meaning of high levels of income for the self-realization process and also the necessary caveat that each of these factors may be occurring in varying combinations at different times, perhaps the only statement that appears defensible at this time and which has any degree of empirical usefulness is that the impact of money on self-realization will vary greatly depending on the salience of some of the factors we have discussed here and that without knowledge of such salience in a specific instance a clear prediction is difficult to make.

REFERENCES

Bartoleme, F. 1972. Executives as human beings. *Harvard Business Review*, 50: 62–69.

Bartoleme, F. 1983. The work alibi: When it's harder to go home. *Harvard Business Review*, 61: 67–74.

Bellu, R., Korman, A. K., Lavy, C., and Greenberg, J. Mimeo. *A Cross-Cultural Study of Personal and Social Alienation*. Baruch College: Paper to be submitted for publication.

Brown, J. F. 1961. *The Motivation of Behavior*. New York: McGraw-Hill.

Chapman, F. S. 1987. Executive guilt: Who's taking care of the children? *Fortune*, April 14.

Crocitto, M. 1986. *Correlates of Personal and Social Alienation in Health Care Professionals*. Paper presented at the National Conference of the Association of Human Resources Management and Organizational Behavior.

Deutsch, C. H. 1986. Women's success: A darker side. *New York Times*, Sept. 10, pp. C1, C10.

Evans, P., and Bartoleme, F. 1981. *Must Success Cost So Much?* New York: Basic Books.

Gilligan, C. 1982. *In a Different Voice: Psychological Theory and Women's Development*. Cambridge, Mass.: Harvard University Press.

Grief, B., and Munter, P. 1980. *Trade-Offs*. New York: New American Library.

Gumpert, D. E., and Boyd, D. F. 1984. The loneliness of the small-business owner. *Harvard Business Review*, Nov.–Dec. 18–20, 22, 24.

Kipnis, D. 1976. *The Powerholders*. Chicago, Ill.: University of Chicago Press.

Kofomidos, J. R. 1984. A question of balance. *Issues and Observations*, 1: 1–9.

Korman, A. K. 1974. *The Psychology of Motivation*. Englewood-Cliffs, N.J.: Prentice-Hall.

Korman, A. K. 1980. *Career Success and Work Performance: Desirable Goals or Double Binds?* Invited Address. Division 14, Annual Convention of the American Psychological Association, Montreal Canada.

Korman, A. In press. Theories of career success and personal failure. *Journal of Occupational Behavior*.

Korman, A. K., and Korman, R. W. 1980. *Career Success/Personal Failure*. Englewood-Cliffs, N.J.: Prentice-Hall.

Korman, A. K., Greenberg, J., Lang, D., Mahler, S., Lavy, C., Omran, K., and Hartog, S. 1986. *Income and Well-Being: On the Relationship Between Income and Alienation*. Paper presented at the International Congress of Applied Psychology, Jerusalem, Israel.

Korman, A. K., Greenberg, J., Lang, D., Mahler, S., Lavy, D., Omran, K., and Hartog, S. In preparation. *Studies of the Relationships Between Meaningless-ness, Normlessness and Powerlessness and Alienation*. Baruch College.

Korman, A. K., Mahler, S. M., and Omran, K. 1983. Work ethics, satisfaction, alienation and reactions to job experiences. In W. B. Walsh and S. H. Osipow (Eds.), *Handbook of Vocational Psychology*. Hillsdale, N.J.: Lawrence Erlbaum, pp. 181–206.

Korman, A. K., Omran, K., and Mahler, S. 1983. *Does Money Buy Happiness?* Paper presented at the Annual Meetings of the Eastern Academy of Management, Pittsburgh, Pa.

Korman, A. K., Wittig-Berman, U., and Lang, D. 1981. Career success and personal failure: Alienation in professionals and managers. *Academy of Management Journal*, Vol. 24, No. 2, 342–360.

Kornhauser, A. 1965. *Mental Health of the Automobile Worker*. New York: Wiley.

Maccoby, M. 1976. *The Gamesman*. New York: Simon and Schuster.

Maddi, S. R., Kobasa, S. C., D and Hoover, M. 1981. *The Alienation Test: A Structured Measure of a Multidimensional Subjective State*. Chicago, Ill.: University of Chicago, Department of Behavioral Science.

Opsahl, R. L., and Dunnette, M. D. 1966. The role of financial compensation in industrial motivation. *Psychological Bulletin*, 66(2): 94–118.

Seeman, M. 1972. Alienation and engagement. In A. Campbell and P. E. Converse (Eds.), *The Human Meaning of Social Change*. New York: Russell Sage Foundation, pp. 467–527.

Slater, P. 1970. *The Pursuit of Loneliness*. Boston, Mass.: Beacon.

Slater, P. 1980. *Wealth Addiction*. New York: E. P. Dutton.

USA TODAY. 1986. International Edition, May 24, p. 15: "The hard part of business—staying alive."

Vredenburgh, D. J., and Sheridan, J. E. 1979. Individual and occupational determinants of life satisfaction and alienation. *Human Relations*, 32: 1023–1038.

Vroom, V. 1964. *Work and Motivation*. New York: Wiley.

Weiss, F. A. 1961. Self-alienation: Dynamics and therapy. *The American Journal of Psychoanalysis*. Reprinted in Eric Josephson and Mary Josephson (eds.), *Man Alone: Alienation in Modern Society*. 1962. New York: Dell Publishing, pp. 463–477.

4

Self-Realization and Adjustment: The Basis for a New Approach to the Problem

Edgar Krau

It would not have been too difficult for modern psychology to solve the theoretical problems of self-realization, but no use has been made until now of the accumulated knowledge which would have permitted the elaboration of a theory in accordance with reality. The reasons for this state of affairs are social and psychological, mutually reinforcing each other.

First, the tremendous technological progress of our time makes the thinking of earlier generations look obsolete and ludicrous. There is a strong tendency to neglect earlier ideas and theories because of the conviction that the ruling mentality in the advanced societies of the twentieth century represents a universal model of thought and behavior, and there is no relevance in what has been said and done in another time or is presently being said and done in another culture.

Second, the psychologist is and remains a professional, and, as if perceiving the situation-stimuli of a giant projective test, s/he expresses his/her own ideals in theories referring to his/her standing and aspirations in society. The psychologist will therefore strive to maintain a theoretical framework in which self-realization (at which s/he aspires) means the full gratification of all his/her needs, acknowledging him/her as winner. People stigmatized as losers are not admitted to this club. Such an attitude is maintained by prejudice-like schemata of what self-realization is. Then the contradictory facts are screened out. In the domain of self-realization several schemata–dogmas reinforced by social wishfulness are in contradiction with the observable reality:

1. The pyramidal construction of human needs allows for self-actualization (the pyramid's highest step) to occur only after the gratification of all previous need-

steps of the pyramid (physiological needs, economic security, affiliation, social recognition).
2. Self-realization is the attribute of a "successful person," the winner in social competition who is motivated by achievement. Only such a person is able to enjoy success and to be fully satisfied and happy.
3. The main field of competition for success leading to self-realization is the vocational field, and the latter represents the exclusive domain where people must prove themselves and realize all their potential in order to achieve self-realization.

The first and most thoroughly elaborated theory on the pyramidal character of human needs is that of Maslow (1943, 1954). The Maslow pyramid consists of five steps: physiological needs, security needs (physical and economic), the need for love and affiliation, the need for recognition, and, finally, the need for self-realization, demanding that the person be active in the field that is appropriate for his/her abilities and do what s/he can do best: a musician shall make music, a painter shall paint, and a poet shall write poems if s/he wants to realize him/herself. Man has to be what he can be. One reaches self-realization only if and when all the other need-steps of the pyramid have been gratified; therefore Maslow contends that not everyone is able to rise to this stage—in his view, only one out of ten will. According to Lowry (1973), Maslow's biographer, Maslow investigated people who he thought had attained self-realization, mostly *university professors* (emphasis mine: E. K.), and he concluded that, as a matter of fact, self-realization is mental health. Those people do not suffer from shame, guilt, or anxiety; they are good-humored animals, full of lust and appetite, who enjoy life, who accept life as it is and do not complain that nature should have done things in some other way. A self-realized person is therefore spontaneous and creative, since anxiety hinders the expression of spontaneity (cf. Maslow, 1943).

Let us for a moment bypass the meritorious characteristics of this theory, for there undoubtedly are such—the actualization of the person's potential in the "appropriate" areas (although we shall give this concept of appropriateness a slightly different interpretation), the absence of frustration which induces the possibility of sponteneity, of creativity. However, this theory was elaborated by following up university professors—obviously with tenure and a solid status in their institutions, the elite of universities. Here is the petitio principii: We get a theory expressing the idealized self-image of a certain social stratum, the one of professionals to which Maslow himself belonged. Maslow did not even conceive that self-realization might be found in different forms in other strata of society. His projective, preconceived image prevented even the occurence of such a thought. He might have changed his mind, had he listened to the wisdom of the history of mankind, but he did not: the 1940s and 1950s were the years in which material civilization seemed to make a giant headway. It was the era that discovered the applications of nuclear energy and also cybernetics, the science of control and communication, thus laying the foundation of the concept of the modern world.

It is at this point that the first thesis of the existent self-realization theory that we owe to Maslow links up with the second one, namely, the theory of achievement motivation introduced by McClelland and Atkinson. This theory attempts to account for the determinants of the direction, the magnitude, and the persistence of behavior in the limited but very important domain of human activity when an individual knows that his performance will be evaluated in relation to some standard of excellence (Atkinson, 1964). The disposition called achievement motive may be considered also as a capacity for taking pride in accomplishment when the individual succeeds in his/her task. Conversely, a person low in achievement motivation acts as if s/he were motivated by fear of failure, showing a tendency to react with anxiety and avoidance behavior to situations in which his/her performance is to be evaluated, rather than seeking and enjoying success (Atkinson, 1964).

To link the theory of achievement motivation to the Maslowian theory of self-realization, one further step is needed. Atkinson writes: "Striving to excel, to get ahead, to win in competition with some standard or other, is generally conceded to be a mainspring of the upward social mobility that has characterized the relatively open American society" (Atkinson, 1977). The implicit idea is that self-actualization and the satisfaction and happiness that follow from it are linked to success in an activity triggered by achievement motivation in competition for excellence in the occupational field, ensuring for the winner upward social mobility. Indeed, there is some research evidence, provided by Mahone (1960), attesting to more realistic aspirations in vocational choice by persons with high achievement motivation. On the macro-level, McClelland (1961) conducted a content analysis of children's readers published between 1920–1929 in 23 different nations. Correlations of achievement imagery for this decade were found with an index of economic growth, based on kilowatt hours of electrical consumption. However, these data may be considered relevant to the problem of self-realization only if we implicitly presume that self-realization has to find its expression in the accumulation of material goods through vocational activity, and precisely these assumptions raise serious doubts since they contradict the spiritual history of mankind. To clarify the doubts, we must see what modern multidisciplinary research findings have to say on this subject. If, despite contrary findings, no serious move had been made to change and accomodate to reality the basic assumptions of the self-realization theory based on the Maslowian conception and the school of achievement motivation, then the dogmatic character of these assumptions would become evident.

Since the 1950s motivation theory has had to cope with development in the need system theory and in the values and conceptions of society. Despite these developments the essentials of the need gratification pyramid virtually remained untouched. Maslow himself acknowledged some incongruencies in his theory, and therefore in his later works he introduced changes into the structure of the need pyramid, as he spoke of deficiency and growth motivation (Maslow, 1962). Alderfer (1969) described a three-step ERG pyramid consisting of (a) existence needs, which include all the various forms of material and physiological desires, (b) relatedness needs, including all the needs that involve relationships with significant other people, and (c) growth needs, including all the needs that allow a person to have creative or productive effects on himself and the environment.

From our point of view there is a definite progress in the definition of growth needs, with Alderfer admitting the possibility that they may be gratified not only in competition winners and in the occupational area. Going further, even failure is acknowledged as an experience that may lead to the enrichment of the personality. Nevetheless the pyramidal progression in need gratification is maintained. Growth needs come to focus only after the gratification of relatedness needs, which in turn begin to function after existence needs are plainly satisfied. Seeking relatedness needs when there is little gratification of growth needs amounts to regression. Therefore *de facto* growth needs belong neither to the domain of relatedness nor to the area of existence. The principal content of Maslow's conception thus remained untouched.

Interestingly, such theories have been proposed despite contradictory research findings. The very thoroughly planned empirical verification of Maslow's theory by Hall and Nougaim (1968) found almost no support for Maslow's thesis. In a five-year-long longitudinal study with management trainees at the American Telephone and Telegraph Company, the authors tested the hypothesis that need levels would rise as lower-order needs are being satisfied, and that the strength of gratified needs would decrease. In particular, it was assumed that in the last year of the research (the fifth) successful managers would rate lower on need strength for safety, and higher on need strength for esteem and self-realization. Nothing of the kind happened. The research did not support the hypothesis of the need pyramid, not even of a two-step need hierarchy. Changes in needs were unrelated to an objective measure of gratification in the safety and achievement & esteem areas. It therefore appears that needs apparently continue to motivate even after their gratification. In other research with samples of women, Betz (1984) found that self-actualization needs rank first both in managers and in homemakers, even though the former category of women may have deficiencies in their needs for safety/security, and the latter category may have more wants in their esteem needs. None of these empirical verifications supported Maslow's conception of self-realization.

Pervasive changes have taken place in the value system of modern Western society, the post-industrial society, centering around the services offered to the public. Knowledge provides the axis for social stratification

(Bell, 1973). Today, the spread of education attains unprecedented levels, inducing higher expectations, and there is a definite trend of increase in professions and professionals. All this produces shifts in the values of society.

As a matter of fact, the "silent revolution" (Inglehart, 1977) in values and conceptions shatters all the three dogmas of the theory of self-realization as held until now. It is true that post-materialist values that emphasize self-realization are contended to arise after the achievement of material security, but Inglehart (1977) repeatedly emphasizes that the gratification of economic security refers to the person's formative years in childhood: people tend to retain a given set of value priorities throughout adult life, once it has been established in their formative years. However, the problem seems to be much more complex. Value priorities are formed in the process of coping with the tasks that confront individuals belonging to certain social strata, and less by the fact that some of their needs had been gratified in childhood (Krau, 1987). At any rate, today it is an established fact that scores of people renounce material comfort or esteem in order to attain self-realization in a life style of their own choice. The Santa Fe Experience recorded by Krantz (cf. Sarason, 1977) is a good illustration of this case. This is the story of successful businessmen and professionals who felt they had no other choice but to make a radical change in their lives. Some became farmers, others small business owners, construction workers, or waiters. They sought for the self not as defined by property, work, or family, but for the individual standing alone, confronting his own being and his own mortality.

In Inglehart's (1977) formulation the modern trend is expressed in more liberal values, in greater openness to innovation, a greater value placed on knowledge and on professional norms in comparison with organizational ones—in short, a delegitimization of traditional values. This latter phenomenon leads to a change in the sense of success. The new ideas about success revolve around different forms of self-fulfillment, self-expression, the actualization of potential (Yankelovich, 1974). The point is that these ideas are new only for us; they are not new for people living in other cultures—in India, in China—and we have seen in Chapter 1 that important thinkers in the Western culture of the past held identical views.

In a book on the consequences of culture, Hofstede (1980) documents that achievement motivation is not a universal category, and that to stress the ubiquitousness and/or the superiority of achievement motivation amounts to ethnocentrism, an exaggerated tendency to see characteristics of one's own group or race as being superior to those of other groups. Maslow categorized human needs according to the U.S. middle-class culture pattern, Hofstede says, and he adds that there is no reason why economic and technological development should suppress cultural variety. What McClelland (1961) proved was only that in societies where achievement motivation is a dominant characteristic, there are more substantial achievements in material progress. In the light of our discussion, material advancement is not the only form of success, and not the one single condition for satisfaction and happiness in life. In collectivist cultures the latter are possible even at low levels of achievement motivation (Krau, 1985). It follows that we ought to reject also the second dogma of the generally accepted theories of self-realization: since high achievement motivation is a universal condition neither of success, nor of satisfaction and life happiness, it cannot be considered a basic condition for self-realization. At best it is related to certain cultural patterns of the process, whereas this pattern loses its dominant character even in the Western way of life, which is entering the post-industrial era.

The change in the meaning of success entails a change also in its locus. Lévy-Leboyer (1986) remarks that success and competition are still highly valued in nonwork activity, indicating a shift in motivation as a consequence of the devaluation of work (in the French edition the author uses the stronger word of *désacralisation*). With the lessening of rewards obtained through work, there is an increase in the role of nonwork areas in shaping personality. This means the crumbling of the third dogma of the existing theories on self-realization, namely that work is its only avenue.

As a matter of fact, we know since Dubin's (1956) research that work is not the central life interest for a majority of American industrial workers. Twenty years later Campbell, Converse, and Rodgers' (1976) prestigious inquiry into the quality of American life demonstrated that total life satisfaction is a weighted sum of satisfaction with different domains, whereby the most central ones are marital, family, and nonwork fields, with work ranking below these. The research also established that, today, quality of life is no longer defined in terms of material goods but through the sense of self-realization.

The same idea has been expressed by Yankelovich (1974) when he spoke of the new cultural trends that gradually transform the work ethic:

1. The changing sense of success. The new ideas about success revolve around different forms of self-fulfillment. The importance of material goods diminishes.
2. Reduced fear of economic insecurity. Economic security is no greater today than it was 20 years ago, but people are ready to take certain risks with their own and their nation's economic security in order to enhance quality of life.
3. Economic division of labor between genders. People gradually accept a more informal, less fixed separation of obligation expectations and responsibilities within the family.
4. The psychology of entitlement by which a person's wants or desires become converted into a set of presumed rights.

All these changes have not made work unimportant, but there is a definite erosion in the hitherto accepted principle that "hard work pays off." In particular, youths not going to college are turning away from work and seeking fulfilment outside their jobs in sport, family life, and various forms of excitement (Yankelovich, 1974). One should not consider all this as proof that people are turning to higher-order needs in an affluent society which has satisfied all lower-order needs. Amid the very high unemployment figures of the last years and the chronic fear of unemployment, such an assumption sounds like mockery. Analyzing the concomitants of the recession-like economy of the latest years, Lévy-Leboyer (1986) points out that youths simply feel that their work effort is not instrumental to success just as their previous career decisions had had no instrumental applicability in a labor market dominated by economic depression. Wilpert, Sinha, and Taft (1986), in a study dealing with the impact of technological change on young workers, state that in a traditional society there is integration between living and modes of making a living. At one time, work, nonwork, and leisure were totally integrated into one system of living, whereas they are segregated in our contemporary society.

One might conclude that in modern society work is no longer the dominant area of self-realization. However, to speak here of a phenomenon that exclusively characterizes modern society would be misleading. We know from the historical review of the problem presented in the first chapter that work never has been the only and unique area of self-fulfillment. The problem is also and mainly: What is self-fulfilling in work? Sarason (1977) develops an idea put forward by De Grazia (1964), according to which one has to differentiate between labor and work. To labor is to be stamped by the activity; the assembly-line worker rarely if ever has an experience in his job activity. To work means to have one's outcome and product bear the stamp of one's capacities and individuality. In this sense work is the normal or natural human heritage, and there is something abnormal when a human being is forbidden by external conditions from engaging in that fullness (Sarason, 1977). This is the path of self-realization, but in the large organizations of our time the individual becomes a bottom layer of a large hierarchically organized pyramid from which he can rise slowly, if at all, while his life is determined by strangers far away. If the individual is by conventional criteria doing well, namely, he is receiving an increased income, is being respected for his knowledge and expertise, he is enjoying a comfortable home and travel—we assume that his feelings toward his work are isomorphic with these "objective" indices, but often this is not so (Gurin, Veroff, and Feld, 1960).

Even these objective indices of well-being are confined to the upper levels of the organizations. As to the lower levels, Macarov (1980) points out, the dull character of work is strengthened by society's policy of job proliferation to avoid unemployment. When the provision of jobs is the major goal, the worker's efficiency, his skilled production, become subordinate questions. The workers know that the work they do can be done better, faster, and cheaper using advanced machinery. The result is a widespread malaise, with most employees working far below their innate capacities (Macarov, 1980).

If the intent is to remain within the framework of the three principles—the dogmas of self-realization theory—then the problem has no solution. Maslow's elitist solution is illusive: the malaise already has hold of the upper echelons. Sarason (1977) vividly describes the "sense of unhappiness, the frustration and the puzzlement" of today's professionals, and he states that the experience of work of highly educated professional people has become problematic in its satisfactions. The only outlet, consequently, is a refuge into utopia. Mitchell (1973) uses a logical construct to extrapolate from the present situation on the basis of Maslow's pyramid. He sees possibilities of either an individualistic society with self-esteem for what one is doing as the dominant motive (the momentum scenario), a "belongingness" society with the emphasis on participating in collective activities that entitle one to social recognition, or a growth society where people will attempt to use all of their potential to the utmost. In this "self-esteem society" people would try to excel regardless of whether the activity requires the application of all of one's effort.

Regrettably, Macarov's (1980) solution is also utopian as he senses that Maslow's theory is untenable. Perhaps, he says, a new fundamental value that does not appear in Maslow's conception will replace work as the central value. At any rate, his utopia is based on the diminishing role of work in social life. This is not realistic, as production of the necessary material goods, the maintenance and development of society's material and spiritual civilization, will always need work, and this work will always be important and its accomplishment a source of pride and social recognition for the individual.

A solution to the self-realization problem has to be elaborated on real grounds. We are talking here of a theoretical solution, because people feel that they realize or do not realize themselves, regardless of what learned men say. Nevertheless, a theory congruent with the facts and the trends of development may become an important tool of conscious enhancement of self-improvement. Since the proposed theory will discard the elitist character ascribed to the phenomenon, it may prove of definite social importance.

It is obvious that from a moral point of view everyone is entitled to happiness, and entitled to determine his/her own form of self-realization. Henry Ford saw his self-realization in the growth of his business, but Robert Owen, equally a businessman, saw it in his philanthropic work. Albert Schweitzer was also not "just a doctor." Such considerations suggest that the area of self-realization is one of conscious choice.

If so, what happens to the "full gratification of all other needs?" History teaches that self-realization has a price. Perhaps only the fool of Erasmus of Rotterdam is equally happy with all aspects of his life. Generally self-realization entails compromises in other areas of life. Beethoven lived in isolation, Schiller in a very precarious material situation, Pushkin under fierce political persecutions; the love life of Napoleon is even today the object of scornful comedies.

We are putting forward the thesis that *self-realization functions within the process of adjustment*. A person will realize him/herself and be satisfied and happy by achieving his/her aspirations in areas of life central to him/her, while compromising and adjusting to existing frameworks in other areas. In other words, a compromise in nonsalient areas of life replaces the thesis of a complete gratification of all prior needs when reaching self-realization.

This first sense of the relationship between self-realization and adjustment is in line with the findings of Campbell et al. (1976) that there is a trend to declare a basic satisfaction with life as a whole, although the domains of satisfaction vary in life and satisfaction is not homogeneous in all domains. For every social group (we may add: for every person) there are more central and more peripheral domains of life, and the general life satisfaction consists of the sum of satisfactions with life domains, weighted according to their centrality.

It follows that for general satisfaction to emerge, even if not all needs and aspirations have been gratified, there has to be an important satisfaction in a salient area of life, and there must be no feeling of crushing misery and frustration in other areas. Our second thesis applies this conclusion to the problem of self-realization and states that self-realization rests on three premises: (1) achievement in the salient life domain, (2) no serious complaints in any other area, whence (3) a feeling of high and lasting overall satisfaction arises, that is, satisfaction with the present situation, but mainly an optimistic outlook to the future. This latter clarification is important. It allows one to categorize as self-realization a situational attainment that may not be rewarded in the present, but is certainly expected to be so in the future. Besides, Campbell et al. (1976) also define satisfaction in terms of the relationship between aspirations and expectations, not in terms of past attainments.

Self-realization does not entail the absence of aspirations. Man has aspirations even at the apex of a successful life, and for the feeling of self-realization to appear it is merely necessary that there be no frustrations. This does not mean that self-realization is only a feeling. It is subjectively felt as happiness, but the latter has an objective basis in the achievements attained in the salient area of life activity. This statement again introduces a problem: the relationship between the objective and the subjective aspects of achievement. Nuttin, Fraisse, and Meili (1968) point out that people establish goals that they hope to reach, but a certain individual's goal may be considered as a failure by other people or in other conditions. Such an individualistic determination of self-realization would make objective investigations of the phenomenon very difficult. Fortunately there is a strong social patterning of individual behavior. The most intimate aspirations, points out Chombart de

Lauwe (1971), always bear the characteristic of a certain society. The individual turns toward a certain object either together, or in conflict, with someone else. Aspiration means rivalry or participation.

Let us underscore the important idea that aspiration need not mean rivalry. Moreover, it would be a simplification of facts to say that all the individual's aspirations are minted by his close environment. Our thesis is that the standard of measurement of aspirations and as such of achievements in the person's salient area of life activities is represented by the social perception of the person's reference groups. In usual circumstances the membership and reference group will coincide, but there are conditions in which the two are not identical. The relatedness of self-realization achievements to the standards of the reference group explains the nonconformistic behaviors that defy the norms of conduct in the person's membership group and are performed to gain present or future approval of a real or supposed reference group. It will also explain the part of social variance in the subjective appraisal of objective attainment. An individual may be frustrated after reaching a certain achievement if his/her reference group has higher and very competitive standards of performance, while another person belonging to the same group and having the same attainment may feel s/he fully realized him/herself as his/her reference group has more lenient standards of evaluation. As such, self-realization and the corresponding feeling are closely linked to adjusting oneself to the standards and the life style of one's social reference group. This is the second meaning of the theory that self-realization functions within the process of adjustment.

The third meaning refers to the necessity of being adjusted to one's job. It has been pointed out earlier that work is not necessarily the salient area of life activity. Nevertheless, in order to actualize him/herself, the person must not be frustrated and feel miserable. Work is very intimately linked with psychological health. Even if it is not one's central life interest, it contains the gratification categories of security, usefulness, status, and belongingness which are important to overall satisfaction. Campbell et al. (1976) have shown that people highly satisfied with their jobs are also more likely to express high levels of satisfaction with other life domains. In our conception there is *no* need for high satisfaction with work for self-realization to be possible in another life area. However, there is a need for *being adjusted* to the various requirements of one's work activity, otherwise frustration and maladjustments are inevitable, and they preclude the feeling of self-realization and happiness.

The line of discussion developed hitherto should not give the impression that the variance of self-realization is nearly all social. It has a strong personal component rooted in the individual's aptitudes and other personality characteristics such as his/her interests, temperament, or character. Society offers challenges and possibilities of self-actualization. Whether the individual will make use of them depends, first, on whether s/he is willing to do so, and, second, on whether s/he is capable of doing so. Some people are frustrated as they are unwilling to play according to the rules of their reference group, and there are others who simply are not capable of achieving any of the goals set by their reference group. Therefore, self-realization is not, and may not be, a phenomenon of universal occurrence. What this theory is saying is that self-realization may be found in any social stratum, and not just at the top. This becomes possible because the individual him/herself chooses the body that sets the standards and the goals for self-actualization. The theory of self-realization within the framework of adjustment confers on the individual the supreme right of choice and judges him/her according to his/her own choice. It states that nobody has the right to decide what is good for another individual, and nobody should evaluate another person's way of life and life achievements according to criteria in which only the evaluator believes. Nonetheless, there must be one single exception to this rule: the moral point of view of preserving human society. From a "pure" psychological angle one could speak of the "self-realization" of Jack the Ripper, Al Capone, Heinrich Himmler—the list is long. However, they all threatened the foundations of human society. It therefore is wholesome to consider self-realization as an application of Pareto's (1919) utility. The famous Italian sociologist required that society creates a situation in which every individual should achieve a maximum utility for him/herself without hurting those of other people.

One last theoretical problem refers to the time of self-realization in the person's life cycle and to its duration. If self-realization were conditioned by the gratification of all previous needs, it obviously would occur later on in life and supposedly last as long as all previous needs are in a state of gratification. In fact, in a letter Maslow wrote to D. T. Hall in 1967, Maslow conceived of a long time period between the emergence of the different needs. In a successful life history, safety needs would be salient and gratified in childhood, affiliation needs in adolescence, achievement and esteem needs in adulthood, and only near to the 50s would the need for self-realization become salient (cf. Hall and Nougaim, 1968). This outlook logically follows from the assumption that needs are ordered in the form of a pyramid in which the highest-order needs may become salient only after the lower-need steps have been fully gratified. If this condition is removed, as it is done in our theory, self-realization may occur at any moment in the adult life cycle when people are happy and satisfied with life because they have achieved goals that are worthwhile in the eyes of their reference groups. In subsequent developments they may add new areas to their self-actualization, or they may maintain their happiness-producing achievements. However, generally it is held that if there is no renewal, satisfaction tends to fade away (Nuttin et al., 1968; Campbell et al., 1976). One may even think of a situation in which the individual loses the object of his/her satisfaction (e.g. his/her job or family). What happens then to his/her self-realization? Evidently, from an objective point of view, self-realization is situation-bound. Still, subjectively the memory of "those happy days" will persist, and as long as individuals identify themselves with those events and remain in a state of happiness (while they know that this situation has passed), they will consider themselves as self-realized, and so will we. In relation to time, self-realization is an absolute attainment, and unless we ourselves waive it, nobody is ever capable of taking it away from us.

It is still necessary to take a closer look at the changes in areas of self-realization throughout the life cycle. The problem has been discussed implicitly as the realization of life stages by Künkel (1939) and then by Erikson (1963), Sheehy (1976), Levinson et al. (1978), and recently by Super (1980). The consensus of these authors is that self-realization is feasible only after "getting out into the adult world" (Levinson), as the youth establishes his/her identity (Erikson). The years prior to those events are years of formation which only lay the foundations for the self-realization of mature years. In Erikson's view, ego identity refers to an individual's feeling of knowing who he is and where he is going. It involves a dynamic process of integrating a diversity of previous childhood identifications and role experiences. At this point the importance of vocational choice and of developing a career subidentity (Hall, 1971) is very substantial, because choosing a vocation is often the first important decision inaugurating the transition from adolescence to adulthod. In the view of Super, Starishevsky, Matlin, and Jordaan (1963), the vocational choice marks the translation of the person's self-concept into the occupational reality. In the subsequent career stages he/she implements and actualizes his/her self-concept.

Hall (1971) put forward a developmental conception of career subidentity. He defines it as that aspect of a person's identity which is engaged in working in a given career area. Developing a career identity which contains a sense of personal competence (White, 1959) is conducive to the experience of psychological success and to self-esteem. This paves the way for self-realization because, in Hall's eyes, work plays the main role in providing life satisfaction. Following this conception, it would again seem that self-realization is synonymous with vocational achievements. However, a more attentive look at Erikson's theory, as it may be applied to career development (Munley, 1977) and the application of Hall's conception of career stages (Slocum and Corn, 1985) permit yet another interpretation.

After identity has been achieved, Erikson's crisis cycle continues with intimacy vs. isolation, generativity vs. stagnation, and ego integrity vs. despair. The meaning of generativity includes creativity and productivity, but also a concern for the next generation, and not only in the sense of bearing and raising one's children. It is the concern for transmitting one's experience to the younger generation, and in the sequence of career stages this is a central activity and a very important source of satisfaction in the late career stage of maintenance.

Would it not be possible for people to consider their self-realization to be in this area of generativity in late years? Obviously, after self-identity has first been achieved (without self-identity there can be no self-actualization) self-realization is possible at every age and in every activity, and there may be transitions in self-realizing activities in various stages of the life cycle.

As has been stressed, the activities of the life cycle are not only vocational. From this point of view Super's (1980) theory has some advantages. In the other authors' approach every biologically defined "season," to use the terminology of the Levinson group, has its self-realization, culminating with a certain critical event or critical process (using Erikson's terminology), but only Super admits that along with these biologically conditioned processes, which produce a sequence of salient roles performed in salient theaters (these are the concepts used by Super), there appears the possibility that in a certain life period different roles may be salient in different individuals. It has been demonstrated that each role salience is related to characteristic profiles of attitudes and values (Krau, 1983, 1986), but the process must be considered a bilateral one, and changes in values and attitudes should produce corresponding changes in the salience of performed life activities. It should ensue that changes in attitudes and in the value hierarchy should entail shifts in the areas in which the person is looking for self-realization and in the means used for that purpose. Since life experience is the main cause of changes in attitudes and values, the determination of such shifts has not only an internal-personal causality, but also an external-social one.

The unfolding picture is that of self-realization being possible along the entire adult life cycle with a "common variance" due to the changes in activities conditioned by the life cycle itself, and an individual variance due to personal emphases. Since self-realization is not possible if the person feels frustrated and miserable, there must be no contradiction between personal emphases and the common variance of the life cycle. Fifty years ago Künkel (1939) stated that life satisfaction follows from the active acceptance of every life stage, with all its constraints and limitations. Once again self-realization is not absolute freedom of self-deployment, but the capacity to actualize the chosen potential within given constraints, including the constraints of life cycle stages. This is the final meaning of the theory that self-realization functions within the framework of adjustment.

REFERENCES

Alderfer, C. P. 1969. An empirical test of a new theory of human needs. *Organizational Behavior and Human Performance*, 4, 142–175.

Atkinson, J. W. 1964. *An Introduction to Motivation*. Princeton, N.J.: Van Nostrand.

Atkinson, J. W. 1977. Motivation for achievement. In Th. Blass (Ed.), *Personality Variables in Social Behavior*. Hillsdale, N.J.: Lawrence Erlbaum.

Bell, D. 1973. *The Coming of Post-Industrial Society*. New York: Basic Books.

Betz, E. L. 1984. Two tests of Maslow's theory of need fulfillment. *Journal of Vocational Behavior*, 24: 204–220.

Campbell, A., Converse, Ph. E., and Rodgers, W. L. 1976. *The Quality of American Life*. New York: Russell Sage Foundation.

Chombart de Lauwe, P.-H. 1971. *Pour une sociologie des aspirations*, 2nd ed. Paris: Denoël-Gonthier.

De Grazia, S. 1964. *Of Time, Work and Leisure*. Garden City, N.Y.: Doubleday Anchor.

Dubin, R. 1956. Industrial workers' world: A study of the central life interests of industrial workers. *Social Problems*, 3: 131–142.

Erikson, E. H. 1963. *Childhood and Society*, 2nd ed. New York: Norton.

Gurin, T., Veroff, J., and Feld, S. 1960. *Americans View Their Mental Health*. New York: Basic Books.

Hall, D. T. 1941. A theoretical model of career subidentity development in organizational settings. *Organizational Behavior and Human Performance*, 6: 50–76.

Hall, D. T., and Nougaim, K. E. 1968. An examination of Maslow's need hierarchy in an organizational setting. *Organizational Behavior and Human Performance*, 3: 12–35.

Hofstede, G. 1980. *Culture's Consequences*. Beverly Hills/London: Sage Publications.

Inglehart, R. 1977. *The Silent Revolution*. Princeton, N.J.: Princeton University Press.

Krau, E. 1983. The attitudes toward work in career transitions. *Journal of Vocational Behavior*, 23: 270–285.

Krau, E. 1985. The feeling of low quality of life and industrial progress: Are they linked? *International Journal of Sociology and Social Policy*, 5: 29–43.

Krau, E. 1986. *Work Values and Role Salience in Israeli Adults and High School Students*. Paper presented at the XXI International Congress of Applied Psychology, Jerusalem.

Krau, E. 1987. The crystallization of work values in adolescence: A sociocultural approach. *Journal of Vocational Behavior*, 30: 103–123.

Künkel, H. 1939. *Die Lebensalter*. Jena: Fischer.

Levinson, D. J., Darrow, C. N., Klein, E-B., Levinson, M. H., and McKee, B. 1978. *The Seasons of a Man's Life*. New York: Knopf.

Lévy-Leboyer, C. 1986. A psychologist's analysis of the work value crisis. *International Review of Applied Psychology*, 35: 53–62.

Lowry, R. J. 1973. *A. H. Maslow: An Intellectual Portrait*. Monterey, Calif.: Brooks-Cole.

Macarov, D. 1980. *Work and Welfare*. Beverly Hills/London: Sage Publications.

Mahone, C. H. 1960. Fear of failure and unrealistic vocational aspiration. *Journal of Abnormal and Social Psychology*, 60: 253–261.

Maslow, A. H. 1943. A theory of human motivation, *Psychological Review*, 50: 370–396.

Maslow, A. H. 1954. *Motivation and Personality*. New York: Harper.

Maslow, A. H. 1962. *Toward a Psychology of Being*. Princeton, N.J.: Van Nostrand.

McClelland, D. C. 1961. *The Achieving Society*. Princeton, N.J.: Van Nostrand.

Mitchell, A. 1973. Human needs and the changing goals of life and work. In F. Best (Ed.), *The Future of Work*. Englewood Cliffs, N.J.: Prentice-Hall.

Munley, P. H. 1974. Erikson's theory of psychosocial development and career development. *Journal of Vocational Behavior*, 10: 261–269.

Nuttin, J., Fraisse, P., and Meili, R. 1968. *Motivation, Emotion and Personality*. London: Routledge and Kegan Paul.

Pareto, V. 1919. *Traité de sociologie générale*. Lausanne/Paris: Payot.

Sarason, S. 1977. *Work, Aging and Social Change*. New York: The Free Press.

Sheehy, G. 1976. *Passages*. New York: Bantam Books.

Slocum, J. W., and Corn, W. L. 1985. Job attitudes and performance during three career stages. *Journal of Vocational Behavior*, 26: 126–145.

Super, D. E. 1980. A life-span, life-space approach to career development. *Journal of Vocational Behavior*, 16: 282–298.

Super, D. E., Starishevsky, R., Matlin, N., and Jordaan, J. P. 1963. *Career Development: A Self-concept Theory*. Princeton, N.J.: College Examination Board.

White, R. 1959. Motivation reconsidered: The concept of competence. *Psychological Review*, 66: 297–323.

Wilpert, B., Sinha, D., and Taft, R. 1986. *Psychological Perspectives on Technological Change and Young Workers*. Paper presented at the International Social Science Council.

Yankelovich, D. 1974. The meaning of work. In The American Assembly, Columbia University (ed.), *The Worker and the Job: Coping with Change*. Englewood Cliffs, N.J.: Prentice-Hall.

5

Self-Realization and Adjustment: Empirical Research Evidence

Edgar Krau

At this point the reader is entitled to ask for empirical evidence that could prove the theoretical positions put forward in the previous chapter.

The research lasted several years and developed in two directions: (1) the definition of self-realization by people belonging to various age groups, socioeconomic backgrounds, and occupations, (2) the use of objective indices to describe the behavior of self-fulfilled people. The aim of the second research direction was also meant to serve as a cross-validating procedure for the findings of the "subjective" direction of the research. Therefore, the two research directions were conducted with separate samples.

FIRST RESEARCH DIRECTION

In the first research the sample was comprised of 56 persons. The characteristics of this sample appear in Table 5.1. It can be seen that Hall's (1976) three main career stages are represented, namely Establishment, Advancement, and Maintenance. For statistical reasons the division into stages is based on decades, but several authors (e.g., Murphy and Burk, 1976) adopt such a division also on substantive grounds.

In the area of socioeconomic background the sample comprises a whole gamut of statuses starting with clerical and manual jobs, then continuing with lower level technicians and engineers, and ending with professionals and people in managerial positions. The educational record of the sample is correspondingly divided into people with only high school education (with or without additional formal vocational schooling), persons with complete

Table 5.1
Characteristics of the First Research Sample

	25-35 years	36-45 years	Over 46 years	Clerical & Manual jobs	Technicians	Engineers	Professionals (liberal)	Managerial positions
Absolute figures	35	14	7	9	8	22	9	8
Percentages	62.5	25	12.5	16	14.2	39.2	16	14.2

	High School & vocational training	College	University graduates	Males	Females	Married	Celibate	Divorced
Absolute figures	9	28	19	37	19	36	14	6
Percentages	16	50	33.9	66	33.9	64.3	25	10.7

Note: N = 56

or partial education in college, and finally persons with full university degrees (about one-third of the sample).

The following research instruments were administered: (a) a questionnaire inquiring about the person's self-realization (see below); (b) a projective personality test based on sentence completion, elaborated by Krau (Krau, 1967; Meir and Krau, 1983). This test measures on a scale between 0 and 4 points the following traits: behavior control, social extraversion, attitudes toward authority figures at the place of work, self-assertion, vocational involvement, the valuing of money, and the impetuosity vs. control of behavior in issues involving money; (c) a variant of the Mehrabian Risk Preference Scale elaborated by Mikula, Uray, and Schwinger (1974). This test measures achievement motivation. The administration of the last two tests was necessary in order to offer an objective anchor to the degrees, the domains, and the definition categories of self-realization that appeared in the completion of the questionnaire on self-realization. Since the latter constituted the main research instrument of this phase, it will be described in more detail.

The questionnaire starts with personal and classification data such as gender, age, occupation, marital and family status, then inquires about the subjects' occupational history. Subjects are asked to define what they understand by self-realization and to which life domain their definition applies. They are invited to rate their perceived self-realization on a 7-point scale, to justify the rating, and to say in which life domain their self-realization took place. The next question inquires whether there were periods in the subject's life with more and with less self-realization. "What must happen in your life that you should be able to define yourself as self-realized?" was the next question. Finally, the subjects were asked to rate the satisfaction with their work on an 11-point scale, and to answer the following questions measuring overall satisfaction:

Are you satisfied with your present situation (please elaborate)?

If you are not, what makes you feel dissatisfied?

What do you think your chances are for success in the future?

The answers to these questions were classified into the categories of "satisfied," "dissatisfied," or "undecided," with regard both to the present situation and to the future. These categories were finally combined so as to yield a satisfaction score ranging from 1 to 9 points, assigning the greater weight to future outlook. Thus, for example, satisfied in the present but with a poor outlook on the future was given a score of 5, while dissatisfied at present but optimistic about future chances received a score of 6. The question concerning the causes of dissatisfaction aimed at allowing a correct assessment of the frame of reference used by the subjects for present satisfaction.

The research showed that the concept of self-realization was familiar to the subjects. Their reaction was quick and animated, but only 12.5 percent referred to a concrete situation ("to advance in my job" or "to build a happy family"). A substantial part of the definitions of self-realization (48.21%) describe a state of satisfaction and happiness following from situations of a certain kind, which, however, are not specifically described. Here is a synopsis of the definitions:

1. Personal development: 5 answers (9.8%)
   "Emotional and physical creation," "Achievements in the personal domain," "Understanding the world."
2. Economic ease and status: 9 answers (17.6%)
   "To live in economic ease," "Money," "To advance in status."
3. To reach happiness in family and love: 4 answers (7.8%)
   "To build a happy family," "To find the ideal life partner," "To see my children grow."
4. To realize one's potential: 6 answers (11.7%)
   "To do what I am capable of," "To contribute what I am capable of and to receive what I merit."
5. The realization of dreams and aspirations: 17 answers (33.3%)
   "To realize my dreams," "To realize my ideas and ambitions."
6. To do what one likes in the absence of any coercion: 10 replies (19.6%)
   "To do what one wishes to do, as one takes the responsibility for good and bad outcomes." "To do with enjoyment what you like to do, to have an edifying job and a happy family that makes you happy."

One may already see that when the subjects speak of self-realization they have by far not only work in mind. Table 5.2 presents the distribution of domains mentioned first in answer to the question in which domain the subject considers that his/her self-realization had taken place (has to take place). The results are nearly the same when looking at the general frequency distribution of areas mentioned, and also at people who rate themselves as maximally self-realized.

It is true that work occupies the first place in both the frequency and preference perspectives, but it is very closely followed by the area of family life; above all, work enjoys a declared top importance only for about one-third of the subjects. Studies, economic well-being, and status are also linked to work, but this link is indirect as far as self-realization is concerned: its main domain of application is not work, and the latter appears only instrumental in achieving certain objectives located in other areas of life. While the importance of work is recognized, self-realization is not necessarily considered as taking place in this area.

Table 5.2
The Areas of Self-Realization Mentioned by the Subjects

		Work	Family	Social relations	Personal domain	Studies (knowledge)	Economic well-being	Status (power)	Leisure (hobbies)	Health
Mentioned first (N = 56)	n	16	13	5	6	4	7	3	2	—
	%	28.5	23.2	8.9	10.7	7.1	12.5	5.3	3.5	
Frequency of mentioning (N = 128)	n	38	31	11	8	12	11	7	9	1
	%	29.6	24.2	8.5	6.4	9.3	8.5	5.4	7.0	0.8
Persons with maximal self-realization (N = 19)	n	7	5	1	2	1	2	1	—	—
	%	36.8	26.3	5.2	10.5	5.2	10.5	5.2		

Table 5.3
The Age Distribution of Self-Realization Scores (in percentages)

Age Groups	N	Self-realization rating scores		
		1,2,3,4	*5*	*6,7*
I. 25–35 years N = 35	35	42.85	20.0	37.14
II. 36–45 years N = 14	14	64.28	21.42	14.28
III. 46 years and above N = 7	7	28.57	14.28	57.14

There is, of course, the question of whether defining self-realization in a certain manner or area is related to higher or lower rating scores. The results show that there is no significant statistical link between definitions of a certain kind and the rated degree of achieved self-realization, nor is there a significant correlation between the height of perceived self-realization and the concreteness of the definitions, gender, education, or socioeconomic status. People who rate themselves as having achieved high self-realization come from all strata and educational categories, and so do people who rate themselves in the lowest category of self-realization. As presumed, self-realization is not the privilege of a social élite.

Significant differences appear, however, in the age distribution of the ratings. For computational convenience the lower rating categories were unified into a low self-realization category (scores 1–4), a high self-realization category (scores 6, 7), while the score 5 forms the category of medium self-realization. Table 5.3 presents the rating distribution into these categories in percentages.

The age distribution of self-realization scores is not a random one. When the χ^2 coefficient was computed after correction for calculating in percentages, the null hypothesis had to be rejected with an error probability of $p = 0.01$ ($\chi^2 = 22.9$ for $df = 4$).

In order to ascertain the measure of influence that age and the strength of the feeling of self-realization have on actually perceived and rated self-realization, a two-way ANOVA was performed with both factors having three levels. The results presented in Table 5.4 indicate that age in itself has no influence on self-realization ratings. The latter are significantly influenced by the joint action of factors, and there is also a significant interaction between the levels of the two factors. The joint action of the factors is significant at the $p = 0.001$ level. In order to determine the strength of influence the η^2 coefficient was computed ($\eta^2 = 0.78$). Since the error coefficient is $\Delta = 0.29$, the influence of the two factors may account for the whole variance of the phenomenon, but at least for 49 percent of it.

Table 5.4
Two-Way ANOVA: Age and the Feeling of Self-Realization

	Sum of Squares	df	Mean Squares	F	p
Age	8.42	2	4.21	2.84	—
Self-realization	240.40	2	120.00	81.00	0.001
Interaction of levels	15.45	4	3.86	2.62	0.05
Joint action of factors	264.00	8	33.00	22.40	0.001
Residual	70.00	47	1.48	—	

As the statistical significance of the findings in Table 5.3 is ensured, we may interpret them as follows. At a young age (25–35 years) the percentage of people who think they have found self-realization equals the percentage of those who rate themselves low in self-realization. In the following decade this latter percentage increases sharply. It is the period in which the mid-life crisis appears. However, in the next stage (the Maintenance career stage) there is a sharp switch toward high self-realization ratings. It is obvious that as experience and achievements accumulate, the possibility of concluding that one has realized oneself increases. Nonetheless, the data show that in every life stage scores of people consider that they have realized themselves. Self-realization is not a privilege of old age. This finding reinforces the previously mentioned fact that people seek their self-realization in different life areas, and each area is salient in a different life period.

As has been mentioned, the subjects were asked whether there were periods in their lives with more self-realization than the previous one. Only 5 persons (8.9%) answered that self-realization is a process and does not refer to a certain period in life. One of them wrote: "In every life stage different things are realized." Half of the subjects (51.7%) consider, however, that the events in different life stages contribute in an unequal manner to self-realization, and they see that the share of past periods was greater. It is interesting to note that as many as 45.7 percent of the young age group (between 25–35 years) turn to the past in search of self-realization ("At the time of my university studies," "When there still was no rigid framework," etc.). In the more advanced age groups this percentage increased to about two thirds: 64.2 percent of the subjects between 36–45 years, and 66.6 percent of those aged above 46, look for self-realization in the period "when I was the general manager of a great firm abroad," "When I still found satisfaction in my job," "In the first years after immigration," and so forth.

These answers draw attention to the fact that when evaluating one's self-realization, one refers not only to events but to their emotional echo. The period of maximal self-realization is one of maximal emotional tension as strong aspirations are *going to be* realized. It is the tension followed by full gratification that appears to the person as the climax of his/her self-realization. This particular characteristic could be witnessed also in subjects who considered themselves as fully self-realized (scores 6 and 7), and they thought that there is nothing more to desire as they wrote, "I have no further aspirations," "Things should go on as they are," "The only thing to do is to sit on one's laurels." Speaking of periods of maximum self-realization, they indicate, "The intermediary period when there was a gap between aspirations and realization," "When I was sent to courses for army officers," "When I got acquainted with my husband," "When I was promoted to a responsible job." It is the moment of promotion, of being sent to the aspired courses, and not the subsequent full deployment of one's potential at the end of the courses or at the job, that are seen as expressing the person's self-realization.

This is not to say that self-realized people deprecate the present, but that the present is an aftermath of "those beautiful days" of maximal emotional tension. The subjects have them in mind in defining self-realization as recollecting "with pleasure all that I have done until now, and feeling pleasure for what I am doing at present". It should be added that the category of self-realized people comprises by no means only professionals, but also 26 percent of clerical workers, technicians, subengineers, and so on, with only high school or trade school education. The distribution is the same when examining the persons with the lowest self-realization scores. Self-realization is heavily tinted with subjective experience. Among the subjects who rated themselves in the lowest category are computer engineers and electronic system engineers; one of them mentioned that he aspires to a more respectable task(!), while another observed that he still does not know what he wants. Half of these people motivated their low self-realization ratings by vocational failure, the other half by personal failure. Vocational failure was explained as a decrease in the quality of life or in social status, and also by a situation that did not allow for creation and development. Personal failure was more often than not related to social isolation or to an unsuccessful family or love life.

So far only group factors have been considered as having potential influence on self-evaluated self-realization. It is legitimate to ask what is the contribution of personality factors. As already mentioned, the problem was approached by administering a projective personality test and a test measuring achievement motivation. This last trait was found to correlate with the ratings of self-realization, although the correlation was not high ($r = 0.25$, significant at $p = 0.05$). In the whole sample the correlations between achievement motivation and overall satisfaction was not significant ($r = 0.18$). This means that achievement motivation is high in people who have realized themselves and are satisfied because they have realized themselves, but achievement motivation may also be high in people who have not realized themselves and are frustrated. The conclusion has to be that achievement motivation is not essentially fostering satisfaction. Since self-realization correlates with overall satisfaction ($r = 0.263$ significant at $p = 0.05$), it appears that the success of self-realization mediates and moderates the relationship between achievement motivation and overall satisfaction. The question remains whether achievement motivation is essential for the success of self-realization, given the variety of ways in which self-realization is interpreted. We deal with this problem in the second research; we continue now with considering the influence of personality factors on self-realization.

The results of the projective personality test showed that there are traits related to the process of self-realization in general, and traits related to certain definitions of self-realization. The first category comprises self-assertion correlating $r = 0.286$ (significant at the $p = 0.05$ level) and audacity measured on the scale Control of Behavior correlating $r = 0.282$ (significant at the $p = 0.05$ level) with the ratings of self-realization. To the same category belongs also high vocational involvement. This trait may appear also in people rating themselves low in self-realization, but it is present at almost every high rating of self-realization ($\chi^2 = 5.82$ significant for $df = 1$ at the $p = 0.05$ level).

Other traits appear at specific definitions of self-realization. Thus, of the five high self-realizers who put their family as their top priority, four have high scores on impetuosity in money behavior. It is interesting to note that this last trait appears in 64.7 percent of the subjects who defined self-realization as the realization of one's dreams, plans. Vocational involvement is high in people who see their priorities in the area of work (75%), but also in those who "want to do what they like" and in those who aspire to a high quality of life. Both the latter categories are high also in the impetuosity of money behavior. High scores in social extroversion were found in some people with family priorities and in some of the subjects who want to realize themselves in doing what they like.

The importance of these results is that they indicate not only the motivational forces driving to self-realization, but also the real motives behind the declarative definitions and the conditions by the aid of which the declared aims can be achieved. Thus, for many people "to do what one likes" does not mean just hiking and playing, but doing interesting work. However, a majority of those who speak of the realization of dreams seem to think in reality of making money. The latter seems to be of paramount importance also for furthering family priorities.

The dependence of self-realization ratings on very personal interpretations may leave the impression that it is hardly possible to translate the phenomenon into more objective common indicators. The problem can be tackled bearing in mind that: (a) people who rated themselves high in self-realization stated that they have no further strong aspirations, which means that they are satisfied with their lives, and (b) work is of paramount importance even for those who see their self-realization in another life area—that is to say, that they are adjusted to their work. It should follow that self-realized people are high both in overall satisfaction with their lives and in satisfaction with their work. Indeed, self-realization ratings correlated 0.56 (significant at $p = 0.01$) with satisfaction with work and 0.26 (significant at $p = 0.05$) with life satisfaction. To avoid the danger that an underlying definition of self-realization in terms of work achievement may adulterate the satisfaction with work criterion, it was resolved to consider overall satisfaction with life as an indicator of self-realization in the second research. This measure was necessary because the heterogenous cultural background of the samples could have jeopardized the unity of the concept of self-realization.

SECOND RESEARCH DIRECTION

The second research aimed at investigating the phenomenon of self-realization in different cultural settings and in the lower social strata, since the research hypothesis assumed the ubiquitousness of the phenomenon. As a result of the previous research it was assumed that we are in the presence of self-realization when a person is satisfied with life and has no serious complaints with regard to his/her work. In this research the influence of the cultural background was supposed to find expression in people desiring, valuing, and achieving what is valued in their reference group. It was supposed further that for self-realization to take place, there is a need for a minimal level of achievement in the field of work, and this satisfaction with one's work, even if the achievements are not spectacular, is a necessary condition for self-realization. If people adopt a new culture, they implicitly adjust to the locus of achievement and to the criteria of self-realization that are customary in that group.

The research was carried out with the following samples. The first sample consisted of 111 industrial workers in a chemical industry plant. The workers belonged to two distinct ethnic groups: 79 of them were Jews living in the town and 32 were Druse, all of them living in a nearby village. While the Jewish urban workers were representative of the dominant cultural environment of Western achievement society, the Druse community, a close society of strong cohesion, has a traditional and collectivist orientation.

The second sample consisted of 83 new immigrants, mainly from the Soviet Union and Roumania, that is, from a society where individual competition and individualistic achievements are strongly deemphasized. Of this sample, 70 were followed up one year after they had settled down in a job. In an immigrant sample this is a sufficient period of time to witness major transformations in attitudes. Because of the strong motivation to rebuild their lives, adaptive changes occur in them at an accelerated rate (Krau, 1982). All the members of the immigrant sample participated at the start of the research in a vocational retraining program organized by the Israeli Ministry of Absorption for new immigrants with an academic background whose vocations were not sought on the labor market. The mean age of the group was 32.8 years ($\sigma = \pm 9.77$) and they had an average length of residence of 23.4 months ($\sigma = \pm 10.20$) in the country.

The research instruments measured various kinds of objective achievements, achievement motivation, satisfaction with work, and overall life satisfaction.

The "achievements" consisted of education, number of children, and the previous month's salary. Because of the inflationary economy which existed in the country at the time of the research, it was necessary to limit the income criterion used with industrial workers to that of the previous month. This criterion could be misleading in the immigrant sample whose members entered jobs in very different settings with different wage scales. Therefore a 10-point vocational success scale was set up for immigrants combining hierarchical advancement during the follow-up period and the skilled nature of the work with the amount of income categories. Five such categories of income were established. The final combined vocational success scale ranged from "unable to find employment" or "dismissed from two or more jobs without finding a new one" (score 1) to "only skilled work with at least one advancement and a salary category II or III" or "without hierarchical advancement but a salary in the first category" (score 10). At the time of their vocational retraining, the vocational success of immigrants was measured with the aid of degrees earned at the state examination ending the vocational retraining.

To measure satisfaction, three instruments were used:

1. In the sample of industrial workers who were employed in the same organization the Job Description Index of Smith, Kendall, and Hulin (1969) was used to measure satisfaction with job facets.
2. The industrial workers and the immigrants, after one year of work experience, were asked to rate the satisfaction they felt with their work on a 5-point Likert-type scale.
3. All research samples were asked to answer the questions measuring overall (life) satisfaction which had been used also in the first research. To the immigrants these questions were presented twice: once at the termination of their vocational retraining, and a second time one year after they had been established in a job.

On completion of the satisfaction measurements, the subjects were asked to note down their complaints. The industrial workers had to do so for every job facet. These complaints were then quantified on an 11-point scale in order to allow for a detailed differentiation.

Since one of the aims of the second research was to test the influence of various cultural backgrounds on self-realization, an examination of national–religious values was performed with the aid of a test in the form of a book catalogue. It comprised 30 titles of books existing on the market and referring to various areas of human activity such as economy, technology, natural sciences, arts and literature, etc. For the immigrant sample book titles existing in their country of origin were used. The test comprised five critical titles referring to the religion, history, and geography of Israel. The critical book titles for the Druse sample referred to the history of the Druse and to the cultural heritage of Arab nations.

In this test, subjects were requested to choose five books which they would like to own themselves or to see owned by a public library. The scoring was on a 10-point scale and took into account the relationship between choices and rejections of critical titles. With slight modifications this test has also given good results in the measurement of vocational involvement (Meir and Krau, 1983).

Finally, the Mikula, Uray, and Schwinger (1974) variant of the Mehrabian Risk Preference Scale already used in the first research was administered also to this sample in order to verify whether achievement motivation is a universal necessary condition or a culturally bound condition of self-realization.

Since it has appeared that the issue of satisfaction is central for self-realization, the satisfaction measures were subjected to detailed statistical data processing by Smallest Space Analysis, a general nonmetric method designed to find the minimal number of Euclidean dimensions for the description of a collection of variables (Guttman, 1968). The statistical significance of this method is indicated by the coefficient of alienation (Schlesinger and Guttman, 1969); a coefficient of 0.15 is generally accepted as indicating that the location of the variables in the space has statistical validity.

Of the 111 industrial workers, 26 expressed a maximum degree of satisfaction with their present situation and an optimistic, confident outlook for the future, while they had virtually no complaints regarding their work. However, all their other characteristics varied widely (see Table 5.5). Some of these people had a low income (IS440, in the currency of today) but some had almost five times as much (IS2,000); some had no children, while others had no less than eight. The same differences appeared in achievement motivation, which in some subjects was at its highest level while in others it was very low.

According to the research hypothesis it was assumed that this variation in characteristics reflects the normative situation of the reference groups. Therefore Table 5.5 also presents the characteristics of the two membership groups of the sample. It was reasonable to assume that in this case membership and reference groups coincide. In immigrants this situation changes as

Table 5.5

Comparison between the Characteristics of Maximally Satisfied Persons and the Characteristics of Their Membership Group

| | Employees with maximal overall satisfaction (N = 26) | | | | Mean group data in the sample | | | |
| | | | | | Urban Jewish (N = 79) | | Druse (N = 32) | |
	Mean	S.D.	Min.	Max.	Mean	S.D.	Mean	S.D.
Children	3	2.72	0	8	2	1.8	3	2.4
Age	34.80	11.37	19.0	59.0	35.83	12.63	27.96	6.67
Education	8.69	2.83	4.0	16.0	10.10	2.85	7.43	1.88
Wages*	1021	430	440	2000	990	465	708	274.2
Achievement motivation	10.11	4.74	4.0	15.0	11.08	4.21	8.31	3.39
Complaints	0.38	0.63	0.00	2.0	1.05	1.21	0.49	0.90

*In the approximate value of today's currency.

they aspire to be absorbed into the host society. We shall return to this problem later on.

From examination of Table 5.5, it becomes clear that the feeling of individual self-realization, as it is expressed by the indices of overall satisfaction and the absence of complaints, makes sense only in reference to the characteristics of the group. While the achievement motivation of the Druse is lower, they are satisfied with lower earnings and have more children. Jewish urban workers who feel self-realized are higher in achievement motivation, have more education, earn more, and have fewer children. One may speculate that the low-level achievement motivation in the Druse sample is to blame for the low level of education, which, in turn, leads to lower wages. However, this is not the problem. Even in such conditions some of them considered themselves as self-realized, and it is wrong not only morally, but also from a scientific point of view, to judge the self-realization of an individual by the standards of another individual belonging to another group. The Druse society has its own way of life, and the self-realization of its members is adapted to it. In this society, community and family occupy the highest preference order and strong links of solidarity appear instead of the competition in the Western style of life. The low-level achievement motivation, with all its consequences, is a social norm in the group to which the Druse sample belonged (see Table 5.6). The point is, therefore, that if people adjust to the norms of their group and have achievements along these lines, such individuals may be fully satisfied, optimistic about their future, and have no complaints: in fact they have all the subjective characteristics of self-realization. The question is, of course, what is the content of self-realization which does not rely on achievement motivation. Table 5.6 answers the problem as the immigrant sample is included in the comparison.

The table shows that both the immigrants and the Druse are significantly lower in achievement motivation but higher in national–religious values than the sample of established Jewish urban workers. The obvious conclusion is that in these groups the feeling of self-realization expressed in overall satisfaction and the absence of complaints and frustrations is not rooted in the height of material achievements. When testing, in a two-way ANOVA, the influence of national–religious values and of success at vocational retraining on the overall satisfaction of immigrants (Krau, 1983), it appeared that overall satisfaction essentially followed the gradations of national–religious values, and only within these gradations did vocational success have a certain impact on the feeling of overall satisfaction (see Figure 5.1).

As a matter of fact, in urban Western culture, also, overall satisfaction is not based on material achievements alone, and social relationships are an important dimension of it. In the present research this finding appeared in the Smallest Space Analysis shown in Figure 5.2. It is the analysis of the Job Satisfaction space which yielded three dimensions with a coefficient of

Table 5.6
Sociocultural Norms Regarding Achievement Motivation and National–Religious Values in Research Samples

| Sample | | Immigrants | | Industrial workers with urban background | Industrial workers from Druse village |
	Code:	At retraining I	One year after job entry II	III	IV
Achievement motivation (means)		6.71	7.35	11.09	8.31
National–religious values (means)		6.56	6.07	5.13	6.75

Mean comparison (F ratio)	Achievement motivation	National-religious values
I–II	7.98*	6.33
I–III	14.23*	35.80**
I–IV	8.09*	2.65
II–III	10.24*	18.81**
II–IV	4.60	5.54
III–IV	19.57	26.25**

Note: Scheffé method used for mean comparisons.
*p = 0.05 at F = 7.95, the criterion of the Scheffé method
**p = 0.05 at F = 11.64

alienation of 0.141 attesting to the significance of the results. The first dimension reproduced in Figure 5.2 is the most informative for our discussion, reflecting the Overall Satisfaction dimension of job satisfaction with Overall Satisfaction in the center of the space.

One can see that next to overall satisfaction appears satisfaction with work and, close to it, the relations with co-workers. Pay, work content, advancement, and supervisors constitute the general framework of satisfaction with one's job. The point is that overall satisfaction is closely linked to job satisfaction, which in turn is closely related to co-workers. It follows that both overall and job satisfaction depend upon the conceptions of these co-workers (i.e. the membership group). They may stress community values, as do the Druse workers, or competitiveness and material achievements, as appeared in the urban sample of industrial workers. Nonetheless,

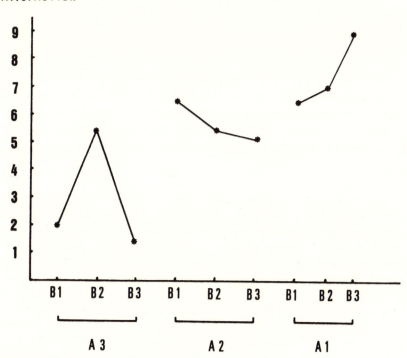

SATISFACTION

Figure 5.1
ANOVA: The Combined Influence of Vocational Success and National-Religious Values on Overall Satisfaction of Immigrants

A = National-religious values;   B = Success at vocational retraining.
1 = Low level;   2 = Medium level;   3 = High level.

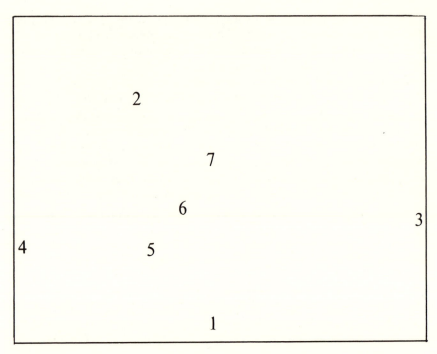

Figure 5–2
Smallest Space Analysis: The Overall Satisfaction Dimension of Job Satisfaction

1 = Work content; 2 = Supervisors; 3 = Pay; 4 = Advancement;
5 = Co-workers; 6 = Job satisfaction; 7 = Overall satisfaction.

the job characteristics of pay, work content, and so forth also frame the overall satisfaction of the Druse sample. It appears, therefore, that a certain level of satisfaction is necessary in all these domains for overall satisfaction to appear. Indeed, Druse below an income of IS440 were not satisfied. As such, for general satisfaction to emerge, a minimal level of achievements in the vocational area is necessary—even if work is not a central life interest. Work plays an important role in constructing a situation in which self-realization becomes possible as it is expressed by maximal overall satisfaction. This is a further conformation of the hypothesis that self-realization functions within the framework of adjustment.

The last question raised by the research hypotheses referred to the change in the "theatres" of self-realization. The problem had been approached ex post facto in the first research and in a quasi-experimental design with the immigrant sample in the second research.

After the first measurements recorded by Figure 5.2 had been taken in the protected environment of the Immigration Absorption Center, the sample, having finished vocational retraining, was exposed to the direct influence of the Israeli host society, a Western-type achievement society. The sample was followed up and assisted in their search for a job; one-and-a-half years later, presumably one year after job entry, the measurements were repeated. Table 5.7 presents the correlations of the achievement motive and national–religious values with occupational success and overall satisfaction at the two times of measurement; comparison is also made with the other two samples included in the research.

When the first measurement was taken in the protected environment of the Absorption Center, the immigrants were still under the influence of the cultural and behavioral norms of their country of origin in Eastern Europe. It has been pointed out that this culture stresses collectivism while individualistic achievements based on strong competition are deemphasized. In this respect the cultural profile of the new immigrants was similar to that of the rural Druse sample, and the similarity clearly appears in the statistical data: in both samples national–religious values but not occupational success significantly correlate with overall satisfaction. As the immigrant sample is absorbed into the urban achievement host society, the picture changes, and this change means a shift in the reference group as they try to adjust to a group of which they are not yet members, but hope to become members by adopting its characteristics.

One year after job entry the influence of national–religious values decreases, and the achievement motive begins to correlate significantly with occupational success. The immigrant sample moves away from the former

Table 5.7
Correlations of the Achievement Motive and National–Religious Values with Occupational Success and Overall Satisfaction (Pearson *r*)

Samples	Achievement motive/ Occupational success	National– religious values/ Overall satisfaction	Occupational success/ Overall satisfaction
Immigrants at retraining courses	0.16	0.43**	−0.21
Immigrants one year after job entry	0.37**	0.30*	0.14
Urban industrial workers	0.31**	0.23	0.29**
Workers from Druse village	0.24	0.47**	−0.06

p = 0.05
**p* = 0.01

pattern of life, which was similar to that of the Druse sample, and approaches the way of life of the urban achievement society. After only one year the process is not yet completed; overall satisfaction is still not linked to occupational success, but the transformation has begun and the tendency is clear. A change is emerging in the area where achievements are significant for the person. It reflects the change in the reference group as new values and norms begin to dominate the former immigrant's behavior. Since high achievement motivation is central to the core of personality (Atkinson, 1977), the result of the adaptive process in immigrants is a change in the theater of self-realization. The first research showed that such changes are common in life, and not merely linked to the dramatic events of emigration–immigration. However, the immigrant sample has offered the possibility of studying this process in vitro under more or less controllable circumstances. It also appeared with utmost clarity that, in this case, self-realization appears, functions, and changes within the process of adjustment.

REFERENCES

Atkinson, J. W. 1977. Motivation for achievement. In Th. Blass (Ed.), *Personality Variables in Social Behavior*. New York/London: Lawrence Erlbaum.

Guttman, L. 1968. A general nonmetric technique for finding the smallest coordinate space for a configuration of points. *Psychometrika*, 33: 470–514.

Hall, D. T. 1976. *Careers in Organizations*. Glenview, Ill.: Scott, Foresman.

Krau, E. 1967. The diagnosis of personality traits through a projective completion test. *Révue Roumaine des Sciences Sociales, Série Psychologie*, 2: 177–188.

Krau, E. 1982. The vocational side of a new start in life: A career model of immigrants. *Journal of Vocational Behavior*, 20: 313–330.

Krau, E. 1983. How important is vocational success to the overall satisfaction of immigrants? *Journal of Applied Social Psychology*, 13: 473–495.

Meir, E. I., and Krau, E. 1983. Some Israeli contributions to the measurement of interests and personality. *Bulletin de la Commission Internationale des Tests*, 18: 9–19.

Mikula, G., Uray, H., and Schwinger, T. 1974. *Die Entwicklung einer deutschen Fassung der Mehrabian Achievement Risk Preference Scale*. Graz: Berichte aus dem Institut für Psychologie der Universität Graz.

Murphy, P. P., and Burk, D. H. 1976. Career development of men at mid-life. *Journal of Vocational Behavior*, 9: 337–343.

Schlesinger, J. M., and Guttman, L. 1969. Smallest Space Analysis of intelligence and achievement tests. *Psychological Bulletin*, 71: 95–100.

Smith, P. C., Kendall, L. M., and Hulin, C. L. 1969. *The Measurement of Satisfaction in Work and Retirement*. Chicago, Ill.: Rand McNally.

PART II
The Means to Achieve Self-Realization

6

Participation Behavior and Personal Growth

Bernhard Wilpert

PROBLEM CONTEXT

Participation, as a concept and as a practice, has been a long and hotly contested notion. Less than 20 years ago an eminent German social critic deemed it synonymous with "the new name of the future" (Dirks, 1969). At around the same time a Dutch organizational scientist called participation the most vital organization problem of our time and expressed his astonishment at the fact that so little and theoretically so meager research had been conducted on the issue (Mulder, 1971). And after 35 years of statutorily regulated participation (co-determination) in German enterprises, a well-known industrialist flatly claims: "Co-determination was an error" (Mohn, *Die Zeit*, 4 April 1986).

Undoubtedly, such contradictions are partly due to differences in a priori value orientations. But in part they seem to be due to the wide gamut of semantic connotations of the very term "participation" itself. For some participation denotes nothing more than personal involvement, such as when economists speak of "labor market participation." For others it means the personal, usually informal, opportunity to influence directly the immediate environment of one's living and working conditions; for still others it refers to the statutorily regulated rights of employees or their elected representatives to information access, to develop their own initiatives, and to influence or co-determine decision outcomes in social, personnel, organizational, and economic matters of their work organization. The latter understanding of the term participation also includes the representation of employees in management or governing boards of their companies.

Finally, for still others, participation means the representation of workers' interests in economic, social, and infrastructural domains on a level above individual plants or companies.

Whatever one's value position and whatever one's definitional preference, the social–scientific discussion of participation will always find itself in a force field of contradictory intentions, political aspirations, and terminological conceptions. While a growing number of recent empirical studies have begun to close the research gap lamented by Mulder, the deficit in the underpinning of participation research with psychological theorizing continues. This is particularly surprising in view of the tradition of conjecturing about participation and its consequences which should long ago have given the concept of participation a special place in psychological theory. For instance:

- In following the work of Meissner (1971) and Hacker (1976), Ulich (1978) sees activities of individual or collective self-regulation in work as playing a significant role in processes of cognitive and social learning. This view appears to be intimately linked to implicit notions about human nature which provide the requisite criteria to evaluate what must and can be considered conducive for personal growth (Dachler and Wilpert, 1978, 1980).
- Managers and organization researchers frequently consider participation as an appropriate social technology to enhance group cohesion and employee commitment and satisfaction in the interest of increased productivity and organizational goal achievement. The implicit value orientation here seems to be effectiveness and efficiency.
- Finally, the consequences of participation for society as a whole are indicated by Pateman (1970, p. 42) thus: "The existence of representative institutions at national level is not sufficient for democracy, . . . for democracy must take place in other spheres in order that the necessary individual attitudes and psychological qualities can be developed. This development takes place through the process of participation itself." Participation is seen in this case as an educational means for democratizing society, as an educational process counteracting heterodetermination.

The context, then, in which the social scientific discourse on participation takes place is characterized, on the one hand, by a high degree of contentiousness in terms of social policies and its intrinsic value-ladenness. On the other hand, we note far-reaching psychologically impaired assumptions about the consequences of participation on the individual, organizational, and societal level.

DEFINING PARTICIPATION

Before going into the possible psychological bases of participation, let us, for the purposes of this chapter, attempt a definition through the use of a mapping sentence:

Participation is
the totality of *forms*
i.e. direct (immediate, personal) or indirect (via representatives or institutional
   means)
and *intensities*
ranging from negligible to comprehensive
through which *individuals, groups, collectives*
ensure their *interests*
through self-determined *choices* of possible *actions*.

The distinction of direct and indirect forms of participation follows the seminal paper of Lammers (1967). It is particularly important, because both forms can be assumed to have differential social and psychological consequences of as yet largely unknown characteristics. The pursuit of interest implies that with reference to participation we speak of goal-oriented actions and not of any incidentally occurring behavior or interaction. The point of goal directedness is further strengthened by the notion of chosen actions, the actors being individuals or social entities. Finally, the gradation of intensities through which actors aim to safeguard their interests corresponds to the general experience that actors are able to control the outcome of their actions only to a varying extent.

The function of participation in its most general sense, then, is to realign decisions and their outcome to the interests and needs of those who are affected (cf. Kirsch, Scholl, and Paul, 1984). In the subsequent parts of this chapter we try to show that a person's self-determined choices, in choosing from action alternatives that control his/her environment, are fundamental for personal growth and self-realization. A psychological theory of participation, however, will have to take into account the interaction of individual prerequisites and the situational factors impacting on the consequences of participation.

TOWARDS A PSYCHOLOGICAL THEORY OF PARTICIPATION

Let us first pursue the question regarding the individual psychodynamic principles that appear to contribute to the emergence of participatory behavior and its assumed consequences.

G. W. Allport may be considered a forerunner in psychological theorizing on participation (1945). Starting with a reflection on the preoccupation of American psychology with motor activities and respective research findings, he points out "that people have to be active in order to learn, . . . to build voluntary control" (p. 121). He continues by making a distinction between mere *activity* as such and "true, personal *participation*." Accordingly, the critical characteristic of participation would be ego-involvement which is fed by a "dynamic factor": the individual's desire for prestige, self-respect, autonomy, or self-regard. This ego-involvement in various life-spheres expresses itself through the individual's active participation in influencing these spheres and is for Allport a necessary condition for personal self-realization and democratic development of society as a whole: *"unless [a person] is in some areas ego-engaged and participant his life is crippled and his existence a blemish on democracy"* (Allport's emphasis), and: *"unless we try deliberately and persistently to affect our destinies at certain points . . . we are not democratic personalities, we have not balance as wholeness, and society undergoes proportionate stultification"* (Allport 1945, p. 127). By his passionate concern with the democratic condition of society Allport's position may strike the reader today as more programmatic than analytic, but he heralds already at that early date all the themes to be developed later on.

A more comprehensive attempt to establish participation as an essential constitutive element of individual and social development was made by Becker (1968, 1971) and Lafferty (1975, 1979). With reference to John Dewey's normative behaviorism Becker develops a philosophical–anthropological position which ascribes an overriding importance to social action domains when one considers the development or obstruction of an individual's acquisition ("funding") of competences. Learning and "organismic growth" take place in the context of these social action domains. Personal well-being, individual action potential, and meaningfulness of human existence are necessarily linked to participation in designing social systems. Participation is an existential necessity. Lafferty (1979, p. 10) attempts to transform Becker's approach into a social–psychological theory of "normative–symbolic interaction":

Participation is a basic human well-being. It is basic because not to participate in the decisions which affect my funding possibilities is to give up that which is *most* essential to expand my control over object–action–symbol possibilities. To not participate in decisions which symbolically control the emotional value (status, legality, worth, etc.) of my action world is quite simply, to choose a lesser degree of humanism (actually a form of organismic sickness) for both myself and my community.

Becker's and Lafferty's theorizing remains very much at a philosophical, speculative level. Not so Robert W. White (1959) in his important reanalysis and reintegration of hitherto developed motivation theories. In a critical analysis of the motivation theories of Freud and Hull and their followers, he demonstrates that instinct and drive concepts are insufficient to explain such phenomena as exploratory behavior, playful manipulation, attention, environmental mastery. The more comprehensive and more appropriate explanatory concept is for White a universal need for competence, its motivational component being "affectance." Affectance motives emerge from all effective interactions of an organism with its environment. Such interactions mediate the positively valued feeling of efficacy. In passing, it may be pointed out that this approach overcomes the traditional reluctance of psychologists to study the interaction of the individual and his/her environment, the interaction with the world of things (Graumann, 1974, 1979).

White's reflections were to have consequences that are of immediate importance for our context. Referring to White it was Deci (1975) who postulated that intrinsically motivated behavior is generated from an innate, ever-present need for competent and self-determined interaction with the environment. It is this very need which makes people look for environmental challenges, which correspond to their competences, in order to master them. It appears that Deci's concept of competent action might usefully be complemented by a distinction made by Bandura (1977): the expectancy or conviction that one can successfully carry out the problem-solving action (self-efficacy), as against the expectancy that a certain behavior will lead to certain consequences (outcome expectancy). A similarly useful distinction is offered by Staw (1982) between the link of a person's expectations regarding the *control of outcomes* (similar to efficacy) and the accuracy of *predicting outcomes* (e.g. rewards in a tightly controlled organization). The different expectations are assumed to lead to different behavior. From here to Deci's more recent theorizing about a psychology of self-determination (Deci, 1980; Deci and Ryan, 1985) is but a short distance. "Control" theory is an individual's experience of having the possibility to choose among different action options, that is, the experience of internal causation (locus of causality). The concept of "locus of causality" or "personal causation" (Heider, 1958; DeCharms, 1968) is not identical with Rotter's notion of "locus of control" (1966). The central issue for Rotter is whether events are perceived to be contingent results of one's own behavior. For Deci the question is what is perceived to be the source of initiating or regulating behavior.

As a preliminary answer to our initial question regarding the psychodynamic principles underlying participatory behavior we may now formulate, with reference to White and Deci, that it is a general motivational disposition to self-determined (self-chosen) and competent (effective) action. In order to be able to describe and explain participation in real life settings it is necessary to expand this proposition with various additional theoretical notions.

SOME ELABORATIONS

The first elaboration concerns the consequences of frustrating the self-determination need. Similar to White and Deci, Brehm (1966, p. 9) assumes for his reactance theory that it is crucial for individuals to experience themselves as sole directors of their behavior. In cases where an individual experiences his/her freedom of action (choice of options) as threatened or lost, reactance will develop, that is, "a state of motivation which activates a person to do everything possible to maintain or regain the threatened or lost freedom of action" (Keller, 1981, p. 365). Subjective salience of the threatened freedom of action seems to be an important moderator variable for the ensuing reactance. The reactance theory has been linked by Wortmann and Brehm (1975) to Seligman's (1975) concept of learned helplessness. Both approaches were integrated in a model in which expectancies regarding control possibilities/loss and the degree of helplessness training represent the critical parameters. In other words, it seems possible to understand both reactance and helplessness as specific consequences of frustrated self-determination and competent interaction (Sauer and Müller, 1980) with one's environment in Deci's sense.

A second elaboration of the basic theory of participation concerns the subjective salience of intended events, which constitutes an important element in the integrated model of reactance and learned helplessness, although not, however, in Deci's theory of self-determination. Wortmann's and Brehm's models share here the well-known weakness of all process-oriented motivation theories, which usually indicate only inadequately the conditions under which subjective salience develops. Without being able to offer a perfect solution to the problem we would like to suggest that a psychology of property (as yet to be developed) might possibly offer at least partial answers. The idea may be surprising. However, we can go back almost a century to draw on an argument developed by William James (1890): property objects, whether material or immaterial ones (e.g. ideas), are essential for the development of the self. Continuous utilization and familiarization with objects leads to an integration of these objects into the individual self-concept because of the "law of mental association of contiguity." The process is further advanced by social valuation processes (cf. Beaglehole, 1932, p. 298). Furby (1978), in her studies of the ontogenesis of property feelings and the ensuing behavior of young children, has identified object control as an additional characteristic: in all groups of children studied the control of objects was consistently found to be the most important element of property sentiments (cf. Stanjek, 1980). In short, the experience of property of an object results from spatio-temporal contiguities and constitutes a context (in the gestalt psychological sense) between individual and object which manifests itself in effective object control (without necessarily being identical with legal property titles: Wilpert, 1983; Thie, 1985). Hence the hypothesis: Subjective salience is a corollary of psychological property titles. They legitimate action in terms of object control and induce reaction in cases where control is threatened.

THE SOCIAL DIMENSION

So far we have only discussed intraindividual dynamics of participation behavior. Mulder (1977) has developed one of the few social–psychological theories of participation as an exercise of power in hierarchical structures. The basic assumption in his "power-distance-reduction-theory" is that the mere exercise of power (defined as determination of other's behavior) is intrinsically satisfying, and therefore individuals strive to expand their power. Up to this point Mulder's approach is easily reconcilable with Deci's notions. But Mulder attempts to show empirically that people in hierarchical relations always strive to reduce the power distance to the next more powerful level while people on that level strive to maintain the power distance to the next lower level. From the intrinsically hedonistic aspects of power it follows that *power is addictive*. On the other hand, if the power distance between two actors increases too much, the striving for power distance reduction decreases due to cost–benefit considerations, and low-power individuals may become apathetic. The hopelessly powerless have, at best, only the chance to develop solidarity with other powerless individuals and/or revert to obstruction.

Mulder's theory presents an organization-centered perspective in spite of its individual psychological premises. His reflections on the individual consequences of exercising power come more as a sketchy afterthought than an important part of his theory (1977, p. 87). These reflections relate to learning processes of an individual, which he describes in terms of a circle: exercise of power → power distance reduction → acquisition of relevant abilities → exercise of power. This notion could easily be related to Dewey's pragmatism and its elaboration by Allport and Becker described above, which would show its significance for the relationship between exercising power (a term which for purposes of this chapter we have used as a synonym for participation) and individual development.

Social psychology has so far also failed to provide a better understanding of the psychodynamic characteristics of representative, indirect participation. This is so much the more deplorable because in our industrialized societies this form of participation is of critical importance. The types of problems which a theory of representative participation would have to tackle are, for instance,

- what are the conditions and criteria for effective interest representation (ratio of representatives: clientele, terms of office, communication structures, etc.)?
- which conditions ensure/obstruct systems loyalty, create identifiction/alienation among constituencies/clienteles?
- what are the individual preconditions for and consequences of being a representative?

From a strictly theoretical perspective we may conclude from what has been said so far that a psychological theory of participation can be considered to provide an important contribution to the understanding of individual and social action in physical and social contexts. Deci's theory of self-determination might serve as a useful beginning, if expanded and complemented by certain concepts of control expectancies, attribution theoretical concepts, aspects of psychological property theory, and social psychology of power and representative relations.

The following concluding section points to some of the most relevant research evidence and the more important lacunae of our knowledge about the connection between participation and personal development.

ACTUAL RESEARCH EVIDENCE AND RESEARCH GAPS

From the point of view of *personality psychology* we may go back once more to Deci's cognitive evaluative theory of self-determination and ask how personal characteristics influence a person's participation behavior. Corresponding to given dominant causality orientations (internal, external, impersonal), Deci (1980) developed a typology of personalities. His typology shows a certain parallelism to Rotter's (1966) internal–external control orientations, which have also frequently been described in the literature as relatively stable personality dimensions (Hohner, 1984). The intriguing question for the present context is whether and how a given personality type moderates the relationship between the energetic principle for participation (need for competent self-determination) and demonstrated participation behavior. Hoff (1982a, 1982b) and Hohner (1984) have warned against a conception of a person–environment relationship that is too rigid and monodeterministic and have expanded the control concept in the direction of a more interactive and variable (in terms of different situations and life cyclical positions) conceptualization. Deci (1980) and Deci and Ryan (1985) have also maintained that their personality classification should not be taken too categorically but rather be seen as basic and dominant (relatively enduring) orientations. They present, however, a large variety of evidence showing that participatory self-determining activities covary with the characteristics of different basic orientations.

The other aspect of the central psychological question regarding participation concerns its consequences. More precisely, from the point of view of *developmental and educational psychology*, what is the relationship between life-span socialization and the experience with participation on the one hand and a desire for participation and the acquisition of participatory competence on the other? Deci (1980) assumes that personality development in terms of establishing dominant causality orientations is largely accomplished by the age of 12. The question raised here is whether it is possible for people to acquire participatory competence beyond that age.

Research on socialization through work suggests that this is indeed possible (Baitsch and Frei, 1980; Hoff, Lappe, and Lempert, 1985). Mulder's (1977) circular model of participatory learning also assumes such learning processes. A more elaborate model, which is quite compatible with Mulder's, was developed by Kissler (1978, 1980). It is characterized by a double helix of interconnected learning processes resulting in professional autonomy. The first helix presents the interaction between biography (career) and participation. It results in participation learning which leads to professional autonomy as the first helix mixes with the second one composed of the combination of factual knowledge with participatory competence (cf. Kissler, 1980).

It is unfortunate that both Mulder and Kissler remain rather formalistic or processual; virtually nothing is said about the content and nature of acquired competences. One of the few longitudinal studies among workers gives the first hints about the resulting competence characteristics (Baitsch, 1985): increase in professional competence and abilities to articulate and enforce one's preferences, more balanced and realistic self-concept, and higher levels of differentiation and integration of cognitive structures.

Greif and his collaborators (Greif and Falrup, 1981) go one step further in their attempt to teach participatory competences to work counselors and employee representatives through role play and simulation of real-life settings where worker representatives negotiate with management. Using an action theoretical framework they try to elicit the cognitive representations that worker representatives have formed through their own experiences. Feedback and discussion are expected to increase the adequacy of these representations in the interest of improving the efficacy of participation of worker representatives. Systematic and comprehensive evaluations of the effectiveness of these training programs have, however, not yet been published.

Mulder's and Kissler's models of participatory learning suggest that we are faced with spiraling effect between the experience with participation and the aspiration level for participation. We could show in our own research that such a dynamic seems indeed to prevail (Wilpert and Rayley, 1983): personal participation in organizational decision-making processes correlates with the desire for further increased participation ($r = 0.35$). Similar results were obtained in other national studies (Gardell, 1977; Koopman-Iwema, 1977).

The most convincing demonstration of the universal occurrence of the dynamic interplay between participation and heightened participatory aspiration levels is found in the results of the hitherto largest international comparative study on participation conducted in twelve countries by the Industrial Democracy in Europe International Research Team (IDE, 1981). Based on research in 134 matching companies and on close to 9,000 respondents, the correlations between actual participation and desired participation ranged from $r = 0.40$ to $r = 0.74$. Gardell (1983) has pointed out that the experience of direct personal participation not only increases the desire for more personal participation but also the desire of employees that their representatives become more involved in more complex organizational decisions which affect the work organization as a whole. Participation and participatory aspiration levels apparently are linked to each other in a dynamic relationship which can be explained by existing theoretical notions. We are dealing here with cognitive and conative consequences of participation that have as yet to be systematically integrated into theories of adult socialization and development.

In a similar vein we might consider the often postulated and studied relationship between participation and evaluative cognitions such as satisfaction. Although research shows that there usually exists a positive relationship between the two aspects (Wall and Lischeron 1977), the relationship is usually not strikingly strong. Evidently other factors must be taken into account which moderate their connection.

One of the—at first sight surprising—results of the IDE-study was connected with the satisfaction of employees from different countries with their respective national normative and institutional systems of participation. It was hypothesized that the existing freedom of participatory action for representatives would be positively related to employee satisfaction with the given system. This was in fact found to be unequivocally true only for Yugoslav workers. However, what correlated positively with system satisfaction was the degree of *legally* possible action for representatives, even when that freedom was de facto not necessarily used (IDE, 1981, pp. 260 ff.). In other words, satisfaction with a given representative (legal/normative) system is not so much connected with the de facto intensity of representative participation but with the degree representatives *could* legally participate! With reference to Deci's cognitive evaluative theory of self-determination, we might hypothesize: In countries with relatively far-reaching participatory norms (e.g. Yugoslavia, Federal Republic of Germany) employees perceive a relatively wide range of action options for their representatives, which, in itself, is positively valued. In countries with relatively restricted action options for representatives these options are perceived as limited and, in themselves, valued less positively even if the de facto level of representative participation matches that in the former countries.

Since participation in work organizations always takes place within given (national) normative frameworks the example shows that in considering participation and its individual consequences (here, cognitive-evaluative ones) one must be aware of this system's imbeddedness, a postulate that is rarely realized in current theorizing about personal development. Dachler (1986) has recently drawn attention to this need for a more systemic consideration of participation by vehemently criticizing the individualistic myopia of traditional participation research and by pointing out that decision processes in organizations are in the first place processes of social construction of reality. Recent approaches in conceptualizing and describing the development of cognitive interpretive patterns in participatory processes may serve as starting points to get a grip on this problem (Staehle and Osterloh, 1985). These considerations already lead from the narrower focus of individual cognitive-evaluative consequences of participation and enter more consciously the often neglected field of the psychology of industrial relations. The by now classical participation study of Koch and French (1948) attempted to prove the conflict-minimizing function of participation. Research evidence today points to a somewhat different direction: that is, the relationship seems again to be more complex: conflicts tend to increase with higher levels of participation and increasing power balance among hierarchical levels (DIO, 1979; IDE, 1981; Heller, Drenth, Koopman, and Rus, 1987). In particular, the higher the influence of employee representatives, the greater the level of conflict in decision-making processes. A partial explanation of these findings could be found in drawing on reactance theory as an integral element of a psychological theory of participation: high levels of participation imply a widened range of options to act which is experienced as a threat to given managerial propositions and, thus, induces reactance which shows in increased conflictuality. This should not be surprising in view of the fact that the main function of participation can be seen in the alignment of decisions to the interests and needs of those affected. Participation is, therefore, always connected with the articulation of possibly contradictory preferences. And it is possibly here that we can identify one of the most critical participatory competences for efficacious participation: the ability to articulate interests and needs in negotiations. Hence, the often-voiced fear of increased conflictuality as a social consequence of participation dwindles to the question of how one is to evaluate such conflicts: as uneconomical, costly disturbances, or as catalysts in the mobilization of resources for solutions to problems and the development of commitment among the partners in conflict to a found consensus.

At this point we must widen our scope to the domain of yet another psychological subdiscipline. A psychology of participation becomes in its widest sense part of political psychology (Allport, 1945, Krampen, 1986), which deals, theoretically and practically, with the equally important problem of the psychological conditions and consequences of acting largely through anonymous mass organizations (parties, unions, churches, social movements). They are, almost by definition, organizations where the principle of interest articulation through representatives is usually the only viable means of interest articulation. The construct of party identification (Streiffeler, 1975) as a mechanism for reduction of complexity, or the notion of trust in experts or of eclectic participation in only a few social spheres (Allport, 1945), are, after all, tantamount to an abrogation of the concept of personal causality. This is where we enter a realm where ground is still to be broken by systematic psychological research and theorizing in order to show under what conditions participation can be an effective means of control for widening or maintaining options for goal-oriented action.

Participation, as a form of self-generated goal-oriented effective action upon one's social and physical environment, may thus be conceived of as a crucial link to personal growth and self-realization. This conception rests on the consequences of participation for an individual's learning and his/her acquisition of ever-increasing participatory competencies through the process of participation itself, competencies that consist of the capability to formulate and realize self-set goals. Personal growth and self-realization, in that sense, are understood as the acquisition of broadened options for choice as a widened and increased differentation of a person's life and action space.

REFERENCES

Allport, G. W. 1945. The psychology of participation. *Psychological Review*, 52: 117–132.

Baitsch, Chr. 1985. *Kompetenzentwicklung und partizipative Arbeitsgestaltung* Vol. 162. Bern/Frankfurt/New York: Europaische Hochschulschriften: Reihe 6, Psychologie.

Baitsch, Chr., and Frei, F. 1980. *Qualifizierung in der Arbeitstätigkeit*. Bern/ Stuttgart/Vienna: Hans Huber.

Bandura, A. 1977. Self-efficacy: Toward a unifying theory of behavioral change. *Psychological Review*, 84: 191–215.

Beaglehole, E. 1932. *Property: A Study in Social Psychology*. New York: McMillan.

Becker, E. 1968. *The Structure of Evil*. New York: George Braziller.

Becker, E. 1971. *The Birth and Death of Meaning*. New York: Free Press.

Brehm, J. W. A. 1966. *Theory of Psychological Reactance*. New York/London: Academic Press.

Dachler, H. P. 1986. Toward a systemic perspective of participation and industrial democracy. *21st International Congress of Applied Psychology, Jerusalem, July 1986*.

Dachler, H. P., and Wilpert, B. 1978. Conceptual dimensions and boundaries of participation in organizations: A critical evaluation. *Administrative Science Quarterly*, 23: 1–39.

Dachler, H. P., and Wilpert, B. 1980. Dimensionen der Partizipation: Zu einem organisationswissenshaftlichen Analyserahmen. In W. Grunwald and H.-G. Lilge (Eds.), *Partizipative Führung*. Bern: Paul Haupt, pp. 80–98.

DeCharms, R. C. 1968. *Personal Causation*. New York: Academic Press.

Deci, E. L. 1975. *Intrinsic Motivation*. New York/London: Plenum Press.

Deci, E. L. 1980. *The Psychology of Self-Determination*. New York: Lexington.

Deci, E. L., and Ryan, R. M. 1985. *Intrinsic Motivation and Self-Determination in Human Behavior*. New York/London: Plenum Press.

DIO. 1979. [Decisions in Organizations—Research Group.] Participative decision making: A comparative study. *Industrial Relations*, 18: 295–309.

Dirks, W. 1969. Der neue Name der Zukunft ist Mitbestimmung. *Gewerkschaftliche Monatshefte*, 20: 385–389.

Furby, L. 1978. Possessions: Toward a theory of their meaning and function throughout the life cycle. In P. B. Baltes (Ed.), *Life Span Development and Behavior*, Vol. 1. New York/London: Academic Press.

Gardell, B. 1977. Autonomy and participation at work. *Human Relations*, 30: 515–533.

Gardell, B. 1983. Worker participation and autonomy: A multi-level approach to democracy at the work place. In C. Crouch and F. A. Heller (Eds.), *International Yearbook of Organizational Democracy*, Vol. 1. Chichester: John Wiley, pp. 353–387.

Graumann, C. F. 1974. Psychology and the world of things. *Journal of Phenomenological Psychology*, 4: 389–404.

Graumann, C. F. 1979. Die Scheu des Psychologen vor der Interaktion. Ein Schisma und seine Geschichte. *Zeitschrift für Sozialpsychologie*, 10: 284–304.

Greif, S., and Flarup, J. 1981. Training social competences for workers councils. *Economic and Industrial Democracy*, 2(3): 395–398.

Hacker, W. 1976. Zu Wechselbeziehungen zwischen Arbeitsbedingungen und der Persönlichkeitsentwicklung. *Pädagogik, Beiheft*, 1(31): 28–34.

Heider, F. 1958. *The Psychology of Interpersonal Relations*. New York: Wiley.

Heller, F. A., Drenth, P. J. D., Koopman, P., and Rus, V. 1987. *Decisions in Organizations: A Three Country Longitudinal Study*. London: Sage.

Hoff, E. H. 1982a. Formen des Kontrollbewusstseins. In S. Peiser (Ed.), *Kognitive und emotionale Aspekte politischen Engagements: Fortschritte der politischen Psychologie*, Vol. 2. Weinheim: Beltz.

Hoff, E. H. 1982b. Kontrollbewusstsein: Grundvorstellungen zur eigenen Person und Umwelt. *Kölner Zeitschrift für Soziologie und Sozialpsychologie*, 34: 316–339.

Hoff, E. H., Lappe, L., and Lempert, W. (Eds.). 1985. *Arbeitsbiographie und Persönlichkeitsentwicklung*. Bern: Hans Huber.

Hohner, H. U. (1984). *Kontrollbewusstsein und berufliche Restriktivität*. Berlin: Max-Planck-Institut für Bildungsforschung.

IDE. 1981. [Industrial Democracy in Europe—International Research Group.] *Industrial Democracy in Europe*. London: Oxford University Press.

James, W. 1890. *Principles of Psychology*, Vol. 1 & 2. New York: Dover (1950).

Keller, J. A. 1981. *Grundlagen der Motivation*. München: Urban & Schwarzenberg.

Kirsch, W., Scholl, W., and Paul, G. 1984. *Mitbestimmung in der Unternehmenspraxis*, Vol. 39. München: Planungs- und Organisationswissenschaftliche Schriften.

Kissler, L. 1978. *Politische Sozialisation*. Baden-Baden: Nosmos.

Kissler, L. 1980. *Partizipation als Lernprozess*. Frankfurt/New York: Campus.

Koch, L., and French, J. R. P. 1948. Overcoming resistance to change. *Human Relations*, 1(4): 512–532.

Koopman-Iwema, A. M. 1977. *Participation and Power Distance Reduction*. 2nd International Conference on Participation, Worker's Control and Self-Management, Paris.

Krampen, G. 1986. Politische Psychologie: Geschichte, Defizite, Perspektiven. *Psychologische Rundschau*, 37: 138–150.

Lafferty, W. M. 1975. Participation and democratic theory: Reworking the premises for a participatory society. *Scandinavian Political Studies*, 10: 53–70.

Lafferty, W. M. 1979, *Participation, Personal Choice, and Responsibility*. Conference Paper, Dubrovnik, January 16–18, 1979.

Lammers, C. J. 1967. Power and participation in decision making in formal organizations. *American Journal of Sociology*, 74: 201–217.

Meissner, M. 1971. The long arm of the job: A study of work and leisure. *Industrial Relations*, 10: 239–260.

Mulder, M. 1971. Power equalization through participation? *Administrative Science Quarterly*, 16: 31–38.

Mulder, M. 1977. *The Daily Power Game*. Leiden: Martinus Nijhoff.

Pateman, C. 1970. *Participation and Democratic Theory*. London: Cambridge University Press.

Rotter, J. B. 1966. Generalized expectancies for internal versus external control of reinforcement. *Psychological Monographs*, 80: 1–28.

Sauer, Cl., and Müller, M. 1980. Die Theorie der gelernten Hilflosigkeit: Eine hilfreiche Theorie? *Zeitschrift für Sozialpsychologie*, 11: 2–24.

Seligman, M. E. 1975. *Helplessness*. San Francisco: W. H. Freeman.

Staehle, W., and Osterloh, M. 1985. Wie, wann und warum informieren deutsche Manager ihre Betriebsräte? In W. Ballwieser and K. H. Berger (Eds.), *Information und Wirtschaftlichkeit*. Wiesbaden: Gabler.

Stanjek, K. 1980. *Die Entwicklung des menschlichen Besitzverhaltens*. Berlin: Max-Planck-Institut für Bildungsforschung.

Straw, B. M. 1982. Motivation in organizations: Toward synthesis and redirection. In B. M. Staw and G. R. Salancik, *New Directions in Organizational Behavior*. Malabar, Fla.: Krieger, pp. 55–95.

Streiffeler, F. 1975. *Politische Psychologie*. Hamburg: Hoffmann & Campe.

Thie, H. 1985. *Zur Psychologie des Eigentums*. Berlin: Technische Universität, Diplomarbeit.

Ulich, E. 1978. Über mögliche Zusammenhänge zwischen Arbeitstätigkeit und Persönlichkeit. *Psychosozial*, 1: 44–63.

Wall, T. D., and Lischeron, J. A. 1977. *Worker Participation: A Critique of the Literature and Some Fresh Evidence*. London: McGraw-Hill.

White, R. W. 1959. Motivation reconsidered: The concept of competence. *Psychological Review*, 5: 297–333.

Wilpert, B. 1983. *Psychological and Legal Property Titles and the Future of Industrial Democracy*. Conference Contribution, Dubrovnik, Oct. 2–7, 1983.

Wilpert, B. and Rayley, J. 1983. *Anspruch und Wirklichkeit der Mitbestimmung*. Frankfurt/New York: Campus.

Wortmann, C. B., and Brehm, J. W. 1975. Responses to uncontrollable outcomes: An integration of reactance theory and the learned helplessness model. In L. Berkowitz (Ed.), *Advances in Experimental Social Psychology*, Vol. 8. New York/London: Academic Press, pp. 227–336.

7

Personality, Self-Realization, and Vocational Choice

Jean-Blaise Dupont,
in collaboration with Claire Jobin & Roland Capel

For many authors, "self-realization" is practically a universal phenomenon. According to this assumption, it is as if each individual person aspired to "realizing him or herself" and tried, to the best of his/her abilities, to reach this goal during the course of his/her life. In some way, this would be the main objective of human life.

This conception of things seems very laudable, and it suggests that in concrete terms we should try as far as possible to foster the realization of such a goal. Nonetheless, the proposition seems, at least at first sight, to consist more of a program of action than a true description of reality.

Whatever the case may be, the concept of "self-realization" initially presupposes another concept commonly called "self-image" or "self-concept." Self-image or self-concept corresponds to the representation or the set of representations (in the broad sense) that a person forms of him/herself. This problematic has apparently preoccupied philosophers (and not only Socrates) for a long time and, more recently, psychologists. Although a careful reading of the writings of both might turn out to be very fruitful, we shall allude here to only a few of the considerations necessary to the understanding of our study.

In the first part of our study, we sketch a few aspects of the problematic of self-image and self-realization, concentrating on preoccupations that pertain more or less directly to the field of vocational guidance.[1] In the second part we shall illustrate them with a series of results drawn from a longitudinal survey carried out in the French-speaking region of Switzerland.

PERSONALITY, SELF-CONCEPT THEORY, AND SELF-REALIZATION

Among the psychologists who have dedicated their efforts and their studies to the development of vocational guidance, Super stands out as one of the leading figures. In particular, he has elaborated a theory of self-concept that has influenced and continues to influence numerous research projects. The perspective of our study is somewhat different. It should be emphasized in passing, however, that if the theory of self-image has always received attention, it is probably because the choice of an occupation conceived of as a means to self-realization necessarily implies consideration of the subjective approach; for in the area of guidance, a subjective approach is required, in our opinion, *by definition*, even if an objective approach must be used in confronting reality, as the two approaches necessarily interact.

Concretely, on the operational level, although the classical approach we have adopted here does not refer solely or essentially to the theory of self-concept, it nonetheless always includes measures of self-image. For many decades, in effect, and particularly on the level of "personality" evaluation—that is, affective dimensions—psychologists have been using inventories and questionnaires of the "self-report" type; yet they have been interpreting in the classic mode, in the sense that the answers given by individuals have been inserted into a model of personality created by the psychologist and not by the subject. It is important to make a distinction between these procedures and other specific ones, in that they question the respondent directly. Such procedures have existed for a long time (Diggory and Magaziner, 1959; Ghiselli, 1954; Lavoegie, 1958; Rey, 1958), though often outside the field of guidance.

If the classic approach commonly makes use of self-reports to evaluate personality, it generally also uses so-called objective measures, and avoids subjective ones, to evaluate other dimensions (aptitudes, knowledge). However, on the level of aptitudes, for example, the average correlation between the two series of measures is rather low, around 0.30 (Mabe and West, 1982). This seems to suggest that the joint use of the two series of measures would improve predictive validity.

All these approaches, whatever one may think of them, are the psychologist's, in the sense that the psychologist makes use of "structures" (resulting from factorial analyses, for example[2]) and invites the individual to project him/herself against a screen that is already more or less structured—which is not, strictly speaking, the self-image elaborated or structured by the individual alone. Any query formulated in an identical manner to all respondents allows the psychologist to compare respondents with each other along the same dimensions; it also allows the respondents to place themselves in relation to dimensions they would not have thought of on their own, but that they accept and may even find useful. In fact, if such partial self-images turn out to be efficient (valid), there is no reason not to take advantage of them.

Some authors contest this view and consider that only a projection based on nonstructured questioning can truly reveal self-image. A few years ago, L'Ecuyer made an assessment of the various positions that had been adopted on this issue (L'Ecuyer, 1978).

From the very start of our work we contemplated testing the hypothesis according to which vocational choice corresponds more or less to a realization of self-image. But, concretely, it was not our idea to design an apparatus aimed at this objective alone. It was more a question of evaluating the relevance of a set of variables already constituting a "model"—a model that included self-image on certain levels—while allowing the possibility that self-image itself might be realized through the choice of a vocation. The assumption was that everyone necessarily has a self-image.

There exist a number of definitions which overlap to some degree (L'Ecuyer, 1978). In our opinion, it is not necessary to distinguish among "self-concept," "self-image," and "self-representation." According to L'Ecuyer, whose formulation we have accepted, we are dealing with a set of traits or characteristics that the individual recognizes as being a part of himself or herself, this set being more or less influenced by his/her environment and more or less tightly organized; to this, in our opinion, one would usually add the individual's feeling of his/her own identity. One could also just as well refer to the concept of *proprium* as defined by Allport (1955): "all the regions of our life that we regard as peculiarly ours," including "all aspects of personality that make for inward unity."

This being the case, "if the self-concept does indeed refer to the way in which the individual perceives himself, then the only real means of knowing it lies in asking the subject himself" (L'Ecuyer, 1978). This logic leads to minimal questioning, applied by several authors with the help of Bugental and Zelen's WAY (Who Are You?) technique, that is, the technique of asking for twenty different answers to the same question.

Applying this technique, L'Ecuyer ran a survey the results of which led him to develop a "multidimensional system . . . composed of several fundamental structures." His system seems from many points of view to be close to certain hierarchical factorial models. In effect, L'Ecuyer distinguishes:

- the *material self* (somatic and "possessive");
- the *personal self*, including the self-image (aspirations, activities, feelings, interests, aptitudes, qualities, and defects) and self-identity (including status, coherence, and ideology, etc.);
- the *adaptive self* (including, notably, self-value and adaptive strategy, autonomy, etc.);
- the *social self* (receptivity, domination, altruism, sex reference);
- the *self/nonself* (reference to the other, opinion of others about one's self).

This constitutes an acceptable distribution—among others that it would be possible to elaborate on the basis of the same fundamental data. But the data used by the author seem too limited, notably for age groups between 15 and 21, and, in addition, the image produced by the evolution of the answers is not convincing enough to win support for the proposed system.

Although this system resembles some other models, as we have seen, its author does not explicitly make connections between them. The same could be said of other authors of the recent literature inventoried by Markus and Wurf. The proposed models are interesting, certainly, but "ignorant" of the classic models such as Guilford and Cattell's alluded to above. Markus and Wurf state that the self-concept must be taken "as one of the most significant regulators of behavior." They concentrate on studies considering "the self-concept as a dynamic interpretive structure that mediates most significant *intrapersonal* processes (including information processing, affect, and motivation) and a wide variety of *interpersonal* processes (including social perception; choice of situation, partner, and interaction strategy; and reaction to feedback)." In fact, they have borrowed a series of dimensions or psychological aspects constructed by others but without really inserting them into a precise and detailed structure—and without indicating to what extent their model is a substitute for classic approaches and models. The classic models may seem too descriptive or correspond too closely to an image of the personality elaborated by a third party (the psychologist), whereas self-image could constitute a dynamic "integrator" more apt to take individuality into account.

There is a gap here, even if one deems it premature to attempt a synthesis, perhaps because the relationships between values, needs, motivations, and so forth on the one hand, and self-conceptions on the other, are rarely evoked in the literature.

In this regard, the book by Royce and Powell (1983) is an exception. Put very schematically, what the authors suggest is that the individual develops *images of the world* (in answer to the question: What world do I live in?), *life styles* (in answer to the question: How can I best live according to my needs and values?) and *self-images* (in answer to the question: Who am I?). These three systems, which the individual tries to articulate in a fashion he finds satisfying, correspond to an integration of more specific systems: sensory and motor systems on a first level: cognitive and affective systems on a second level; and "stylistic" (including, for example, Witkin's cognitive styles) and evaluative (values and interests) systems on a third level. Self-images are derived in particular from the interaction between the "stylistic" and evaluative systems. While these two systems are influenced by the environment, they tend to become stabilized over time.

In Royce and Powell's view, self-images can be observed via two different sorts of approaches. The first includes factorial analyses which reveal factors, within the affective system in particular, where reference to self is obvious: self-sentiment, self-sufficiency, and ego strength. The second includes pinpointing the role of the "self" in the general processes of decision, "personification" (awareness of one's own actions, elaboration of information relating to oneself that is expressed, for example in statements like, "I am the kind of person who . . .," etc.), evaluation, adaptation, and insight.

Making use of the results of numerous factorial analyses or, when they were lacking, results obtained by other methods, Royce and Powell identified some 185 first-order dimensions, 50 second-order dimensions, and 16 third-order dimensions. This would allow a complete profile of the personality, with the self-image appearing in several different ways at each level. It remains difficult, however, to distinguish between the concepts of self and personality. The authors, nonetheless, reserve the term personality for the total psychological system, that is to say, the supra-system. There are no equivalent systems for the self since there are no explicit structural components like those that are applied to the personality (and to its own systems containing components); since the self is personal awareness, evaluation and dynamism (process), personality and self are co-extensive. While the self constitutes a concept necessary to the building of a theory of the integrative personality, it nonetheless remains a rather vague entity—and Royce and Powell rightly wonder about the concept's practicability in the area of scientific psychology.

The problem may reside in the fact that there is an essential difference between the self-image of an individual person, even the one he communicates to another, and the statistical self-image that the researcher constructs after having questioned a set of persons. Even when researchers use the minimal questioning of the WAY type, they then, like L'Ecuyer for example, proceed by induction and elaborate a "model" or "average" representation, which, in all likelihood, does not correspond to any particular representation or individuality. It is a kind of personality theory constructed by specialists on the basis of answers provided by laymen—that is to say, an implicit theory. Such theories are distinguished from explicit theories of the self-image (Markus and Wurf, 1987) mainly by the mode of questioning and the mode of approach (hypothetico-deductive); and each is distinguished in its turn from the classic theories by the perspective it adopts, more subjective in looking for the self-image, yet more objective otherwise.

To return to Royce and Powell, when they speak of person/situation interactions, they evoke the concept of *situational template*, that is, the profile of the psychological "requirements" necessary for a subject to adapt in a specifiable situation. Briefly, psychological functioning is adequate in these terms when the personal profile corresponds to the sitational profile. This general proposition has been advanced for a long time now in literature on the objectives of vocational guidance. In fact, the correspondence aimed for is only rarely achieved; there remains a whole range of mismatches among the profiles. According to Royce and Powell, the most usual mismatches occur with individuals whose functioning in their occupational activity or given career is below average. These individuals have all the necessary potential (sensorial, cognitive, and motor) and the required temperament (affect, style, and values) but fail to use them in an optimal way. Other common mismatches are occupational misfits, individuals who have neither the potential nor the temperament required to meet their tasks.

Since no particular type of personality is ever perfectly matched with the demands of a situation, it follows that some compensatory functioning appears as an inevitable characteristic of normal functioning. In several cases under consideration, the adaptation consists of changing situations. In other cases, the subject "makes do" with the situation by bringing mechanisms of accommodation and assimilation to bear. The normative match also comes into play here—that is, the degree to which a norm (e.g. the plans made with a view to reaching a goal) and feedback from the environment match. This match is treated in the same way as the preceding one.

Royce and Powell's conception—which is very classic on several points as well as in the dimensions it considers—can serve as a general reference or framework because it integrates interesting though partial perspectives. In placing the models of self-image and self-realization jointly within the same supra-system, we must also emphasize the limits of these models. Indeed, in our opinion neither all behaviors nor even all occupational behaviors appear to be reducible at this stage to such descriptions and explanations. This is all the more true since the theorists of self-concept who work outside the area of vocational guidance pay very little attention to occupational dimensions. Markus and Wurf (1987) and even Burns (1979) are cases in point when they cite various works without drawing the necessary conclusions.[3] Next to such oversights, the opinion of Rosenberg (1957), though excessive, constitutes a happy counterbalance: "Asking an individual what he expects from his work is to a great extent asking him what he expects from life." In the same perspective, but more specifically, we should remember the overall evaluation made by Osipow (1983). After referring to a whole series of studies dating primarily from before 1970,[4] Osipow concludes: "Overall, considerable convincing research data exist to support the notion that self-concept plays an important role in occupational preference." He goes on to say that "most of the findings of research support the idea that occupational choice represents the implementation of the self-concept." Osipow nonetheless draws attention to the necessity of evolving "additional conceptual links relating self- and occupational concepts."

Although Osipow's conclusion supports the thesis of realizing self-image through occupational choice and activity, these studies should be pursued for the following reasons:

1.   The studies Osipow refers to concern only North America. Would similar results be found elsewhere, in another environment, such as, in this case, a region in Western Europe?
2.   The studies in the inventory are already slightly outdated. Without suggesting that the corpus should be renewed completely, shouldn't more recent surveys be considered, as examples at least?
3.   The inventories studies can practically all be placed in the perspective of a specific problematic, that of self-image. What would happen if a broader framework were referred to and various data were extracted, among which self-image was not the only reference?

EMPIRICAL ILLUSTRATION:
THE EXAMPLE OF A LONGITUDINAL STUDY
ABOUT VOCATIONAL CHOICE

Having specified the context within which the present research is situated, let us define some of the study's fundamental characteristics.

1.   In trying to determine the principal parameters of dimensions that may influence the origin of vocational choice, we have selected a set of variables that are consistent with Royce and Powell's model, though representing only a part of their model.
2.   Since our goal was to describe the origin of the choice, we did not limit our hypotheses to the view that occupational activity corresponds essentially to the realization of self-image. Nor did we simply take self-realization to be more or less the principal goal of life.
3.   The survey concerns two samples of respondents belonging to a scholastically privileged population, that is, students who are about to finish their secondary schooling (*bacheliers*: similar to *Abiturienten*, *Maturanden*, college-preparatory high-school seniors, A-level candidates) and have the possibility of going on to the university.
4.   The survey is a longitudinal one. The subjects of the first sample (Panel 1, $N = 519$) took part in three series of information gathering (1974, 1975, 1976) before finishing school, that is, before the moment of effective decision-making (1976). They replied later to three follow-ups (1977, 1979, 1982) which were designed to determine their situation (training and/or activity engaged in). The subjects of the second sample (Panel 2, $N = 197$) took part twice in information gathering before the end of their secondary studies (1977, 1979) and replied to two later follow-ups (1980, 1982).[5]
5.   At the beginning of the study, the average age of the respondents was 16. The study of the initial stages of vocational choice thus began about two years before the end of secondary school. In our experience, the problem of choice (its explicit origin) is not a matter of great concern to respondents of the same scholastic category at an earlier age.

In adopting the hypothesis that vocational choice (or, the choice of initial training or education) constitutes a (privileged?) mode of self-realization, it is reasonable to assume simultaneously that the choice and the realization are largely based upon self-images or self-representation.

Although it is generally accepted that each individual disposes of a series of self-images or self-representations, there is less certainty about whether each individual seeks to realize these self-images in his or her occupational activity. Although this goal may seem desirable to many, it is not necessarily the main goal of everyone, even if exception is made of certain types of individuals (delinquents, drug addicts, ethnic and other "minorities"). Indeed, what counts above all is the search for happiness, evoked again recently by Perloff (1987) citing John Stuart Mill: "According to Mill, because happiness is the sole end of human action, the promotion of happiness is the test by which to judge all human conduct." This brief reminder of a rather banal (but perhaps fundamental) "philosophy" aims simply at affirming that the individual can have other goals in life than self-realization through his or her occupation alone. Stated in this way, the thesis appears excessive and corresponds to a hypertrophy of occupation in relation to other values and goals.

This being given, and taking into account the apparatus set up in our study, our aim was to extract information that could illustrate the thesis and even show its limits and significance. This was done by operating on the basis of a limited sample of variables as described in Table 7.1, to which the respondents' opinions on a small number of problems (ad hoc questionnaire) were added.

Reference will first be made to the ad hoc questionnaire (not reproduced here). From it we have extracted data relating to *the respondents' reactions and attitudes toward the problematic of vocational choice*. Although we have taken differences between the sexes into account when they were very noticeable, our comments below reflect the most obvious results that need no statistical processing.

We will then examine more specifically the evolution and validity of variables expressing self-image.

It is apparent that when the participants are questioned on *personal factors considered as essential for choosing an occupation* (Table 7.2, A), factors expressing the psychological aspects of self are mentioned overwhelmingly (with a rate of 96% for interests and tastes) or widely (with rates of about 60% for aptitudes and temperament), whereas acquired knowledge and physical condition are disregarded. At the same time, these participants place much less importance on *environmental factors* (Table 7.2, B). The most highly regarded of these factors—the job market and employment opportunities—is judged as essential by only a third of the respondents (32%); all the other factors appear as "essential" at rates of under 20%. In our opinion, the discrepancy between the two series of factors is due not only to the fact that we are dealing with a privileged sample

Table 7.1
List of Instruments and Dimensions Considered (Panel 1)

- **HOLLAND'S personal inventory:** (evaluation of interests of occupational "personality"): an instrument composed of several parts or modes of approach (self-definition with the help of adjectives; self-assessment; identification with a model, valued or rejected activities, explicit vocational choice, assessment of performances, etc.; the 6 scales allow an apprehension of the individual according to the typology proposed by HOLLAND: realistic (R), investigative (I), artistic (A), social (S), entrepreneurial (E), conventional (C) (DUPONT, 1979).

- **List of occupations:** (evaluation of occupational interests): an instrument composed of 155 names of occupations towards each of which the respondants express their attitude (attraction or interest, indifference, aversion: different factorial analyses resulted in the elaboration of 11 scales: management/commerce; legal, political; technical, mecanical; sports and adventure; laboratory science; medical, paramedical; psychosocial; nature, handicrafts; study of the environment (sciences); fine arts; dramatic arts and the medias) (BERTHOUD, 1983).

- **Leisure activities:** (evaluation of extraoccupational interests): a list composed of around 30 items from which 7 factors are extracted: literary and artistic culture; science and technique; manual work and crafts; political and social; sports; recreation; banal amusements.

- **Occupational values:** an inventory composed of 40 items corresponding to 5 factors: status; security versus innovation; autonomy versus the sense of responsability; well-being (versus prestige); ideology versus self-realization (DUPONT & LERESCHE, 1981-1982).

- **Personality:** (GOUGH's Adjective Check List (A.C.L.) as adapted to French by GENDRE): self report with the help of a list including 300 adjectives from which 5 scales are inferred: stability; social contact; extroversion; independence; anxiety (GENDRE & OGAY, 1973).

- **Self-assessment of aptitudes:** (subjective measure of aptitudes): a list composed of 26 items from which 5 factors are extracted: verbal and psychological; control, management; scientific, numeric; concrete, artistic; auditory, musical.

- **Stream:** the stream - classical (Latin), scientific, or modern languages - each respondent followed in secondary school.

- **Scholastic performance:** marks (final marks for the baccalauréat diploma) for the three main subjects the three streams had in common: mother tongue (French); foreign language (German); mathematics.

- **Plans:** plans as articulated in reply to 3 specific questions about them and broken down into the following categories: undetermined; engineering or architecture; university research; medical; paramedical; non-university social service; arts; law, political science; business school (economics); social sciences; artistic; other occupations.

N.B.: The list does not include certain instruments that were used, notably CRITES' "occupational attitudes" inventory (occupational maturity) which turned out not to be adapted to our situation (BALLIF, 1980) and certain aptitude tests applied only to a fraction of the sample.

Table 7.2
Factors Likely to Influence Occupational Choice: The Opinion of Diploma Candidates

		PANEL 2, (1979) (N = 197)
A.	Factors considered on the <u>purely personal level</u> in choosing an occupation	
	One's own	
	... aptitudes or capacities	54.8*
	... interests and tastes	95.9
	... knowledge in the area	15.7
	... character and temperament	60.9
	... health and physical condition	19.3
B.	External factors considered <u>on a more general level</u> in choosing an occupation	
	... the economic situation	17.8
	... the cost of studies	14.7
	... the job market, employment opportunities	31.5
	... the risk of unemployment	17.8**
	... one's region of residence	5.1
	... the political situation	3.5
	... the risk of war	3.5
	... work-related accidents	1.5
	... ecological problems	3.5

Note: Rates in percent.
*The rates correspond to the relative frequency of the respondents judging the factor to be "essential" in the given perspective.
* *In Switzerland the unemployment rate is around 1.0%, thus negligible.

living in a "land of plenty," but rather it underscores the preponderance of subjective factors.

This evaluation is corroborated by the evolution of *motives cited concerning contemplated occupations* (Table 7.3), that is, motives behind the subjects' plans. Once again it is the psychological aspects that loom in the foreground, and in practically the same proportions. Interest is mentioned massively (94% to 97%), and aptitudes ("I think I can be successful in it") are widely mentioned (about 60%). The possibility of working abroad (45% to 54%) and, to a lesser degree, helpfulness to others (31%) are also noteworthy. The other factors are deemed much less important, for both panels, and differences between the sexes (which have not been formally indicated) are negligible. Obviously, this does not mean that these various factors exert no influence on decision-making, but simply that they are minimized on the subjective level.

The subjective importance of these same factors also appears in another way under the scrutiny of an inventory devoted to *occupational values* (Table 7.4). The items that explicitly express self-realization (make full use of my aptitudes; develop and fulfill myself) have been selected by over

Table 7.3
Motives Cited by the Respondents on the Eve of Their Diploma Concerning the Occupation/s Contemplated

		Panel 1 (1976) (N = 403)	Panel 2 (1979) (N = 153)
1.	out of interest for the field(s)	94.0%	96.7%
2. *	under my parents' pressure	2.0	--
	on the advice of my parents	--	9.8
3.	I can't see any other(s) that suits/ suit me	25.8	18.3
4.	to have a good position	17.1	19.0
5.	I think I can be successful at it/them	60.3	61.4
6.	because it/they would allow me to earn a living relatively quickly	8.9	7.8
7.	because it is/they are particularly useful in the region I live in	6.0	11.1
8.	because I could practice it/them abroad as well	44.7	54.2
9.	because it is the occupation of someone I greatly admire	6.0	8.5
10.	because it is my father's/my mother's occupation	3.7	1.3
11.	out of family tradition	1.7	--
12. *	to help my fellow-man	--	31.4
13. *	to have considerable free time	--	22.9
14. *	on the advice of a vocational guidance counselor	--	1.3 **

Note: Rates in percent.
*The wording adopted for Panel 2 was different from that of Panel 1.
Items 12, 13 and 14 were not submitted to Panel 1 subjects.
* *Yet 60.4% of the students had consulted a counselor and 25.2% affirm that they had received useful help.

Table 7.4
The Attraction of a Few Items Relating to Self-Realization

Items (sometimes in slightly abbreviated form)	PANEL 1 (1979) (N = 519)
1. Make full use of my aptitudes	82.9 **
2. Develop and fulfill myself	74.9
9. Work autonomously	65.7
21. Be able to organize my time freely	64.7
13. Take initiatives	63.6
8. Create something new or put my own ideas into practice	61.8
12. Have responsabilities	56.0
10. Do nothing that would go against my ideas	51.0

Note: Rates in percent
*An excerpt of a 40-item inventory borrowing widely from MIQ (Gay, Weiss, et al.) and from VWI (Super), based on Dupont, Leresche, et al. (1981–1982).
* *The rates indicate the frequency of the choices.

three-quarters of the respondents, while the other items that directly involve the individual are often chosen too, with rates varying between 50% and 65%. With the exception of a small number of items relating to the psychological climate of the work place (also widely selected)[6], the other values (job stability, social esteem, etc.) seem less attractive—and less important (Dupont, Leresche, et al., 1981–1982).

Given the rank attributed to self-realization in the hierarchy of occupational values, the participants' answers about the *importance of future occupational life* (Table 7.5) come as no surprise. About 20% of the subjects, men and women, consider that it is the most important sphere of life, and about 10% consider that there are other spheres that are more important, with the majority (reaching rates between 52% and 67% depending on the subgroup[7]) adopting an intermediary position.

Although occupational life is judged to be important, the choice made at the end of secondary school is not perceived as irrevocable. This is clear in Table 7.6 on the *reversibility of the decision about the initial vocational choice*. The first thing to note is the high rate of subjects who consider their initial choice to be modifiable, and modifiable according to their personal evolution, that is—once again—according to factors essentially linked to the self. External factors appear to be negligible. It should also be noted that in this area there are noticeable differences between the sexes, with women declaring themselves much less bound by their first commitment.

These various attitudes should be considered in parallel with attitudes toward *interference between the occupational life and the family life of women* (Table 7.7). It should be noted that the authors worded the questions of this survey as if only women were directly concerned by the problem of family in relation to occupation, while men remained a third party. The questions reflect in concrete terms a mentality that is rather widespread in Western Europe. But the rates of response reveal noticeable differences between young men and young women concerning women's family and occupational roles. Whereas under 20% of the women would like to stop their professional activity at the time of their marriage or the birth of their first child, more than 40% of the men would like to have their wives stop work. Conversely, whereas a majority of the women (over 60%) replied in favor of a temporary cessation of their activity when they become mothers, under 30% of the men chose this solution of their own couples. Similar tendencies appear in Panel 1.[8]

Table 7.5
Importance of Future Occupational Life as Perceived on the Eve of the Diploma

		PANEL 1 (1976) (N = 306) (N = 213)			PANEL 2 (1979) (N = 85) (N = 112)		
		M	F	T	M	F	T
1.	It's the most important sphere in life	32.4	23.0	28.5	20.0	22.3	21.3
2.	It's an important sphere but no more than some others	52.0	66.7	58.0	62.4	65.2	64.0
3.a	There are other spheres that are more important	--	--	--	9.4	9.8	9.6
3.b	It's not an important sphere	2.0	2.8	2.3	1.2	0.9	1.0
4.	I don't know	12.4	7.0	10.2	7.1	1.8	4.1
5.	No answer	1.3	0.5	1.0	0.0	0.0	0.0

Note: Rates in percent. The form of the question asked was: "What importance do you give at this moment to your future occupational life? (One answer only.)" The subjects of Panel 1 did not answer question 3b which did not appear in the 1976 survey.
Chi-square in 1976 = 13.268, significant at the 0.01 level.
Chi-square in 1979 = 3.492, nonsignificant.

Table 7.6

Evaluation of the "Reversibility" of the Decision Concerning the Initial Effective Vocational Choice

		PANEL 1 (1976) (N = 306) (N = 213)			PANEL 2 (1979) (N = 85) (N = 112)		
		M	F	T	M	F	T
1.	is irrevocable and requires my life-long commitment	12.1	3.3	8.5	11.8	6.3	8.6
2.	commits me for a long time, but not for life	20.3	16.9	18.9	29.4	12.5	19.8
3.	I can modify in relation to my personal evolution	56.9	67.6	61.3	50.6	72.3	62.9
4.	I can modify in relation to external circumstances	9.5	10.8	10.0	7.1	8.0	7.6
5.	No answer	1.3	1.4	1.3	1.2	0.9	1.0

In choosing an occupation now or soon (or the training or education that will lead to it) I am making a decision that (one answer only):

Note: Rates in percent
Chi-Square in 1976 = 14.829, significant at the .01 level
Chi-square in 1979 = 12.410, significant at the .05 level.

The primary conclusion we can draw from these data is that if 20% of the women wish to stop work for family reasons and 60% wish to reconcile work and family, then self-realization does not have to be accomplished solely through occupational channels, or solely through the family.

The questions about the *interference between occupational and family life* were not identical for Panel 1 (Table 7.8) and Panel 2. Rigorous comparisons therefore cannot be made between the panels. But the data suggest interpretations that would tend to confirm those we have made above.

As women—at the present moment—are probably less attracted to occupational life than are men, women react very differently from men in the interests they express, and in their *occupational interests* in particular.

Table 7.7

Interference between Occupational Life and Family Life for Women: The Opinion of Young Women and Young Men (Panel 2, 1979)

(Question asked: How do you envisage the future from the point of view of family life?)

A)	Answers given by women (N = 112)	
1.	I would like to stop all professional acitvity as soon as I marry	1.8%
2.	I would like to stop work upon the birth of a child	16.1%
3.	I would like to interrupt my professional activity temporarily as long as my children are not in school	61.6%
4.	I would like to work as long as possible (taking in help to take care of the children if necessary)	2.7%
5.	Whatever my situation might be, I do not envisage interrupting my professional activity	11.6%
6.	No answer	6.3%

B)	Answers given by men (N = 85)	
1.	I would like my wife to stop all professional activity as soon as we marry	4.7%
2.	I would like my wife to stop working upon the birth of our first child	36.5%
3.	I would like my wife to interrupt all professional activity temporarily as long as the children are not in school	29.4%
4.	I would like my wife to work as long as possible (taking in help to care for the children if necessary)	3.5%
5.	Whatever our situation might be, I do not envisage that my wife would interrupt her professional activity	11.8%
6.	No answer	14.1%

Table 7.8
Interference between Occupational Life and Family Life: The Opinion of Girls and Boys (Panel 1, 1975)

Do you think that: a) for a woman ...

b) for a man ...

		(N = 213)		(N = 306)	
		F		**M**	
		a)	b)	a)	b)
1)	Her professional activity should be the most important	4.3	13.5	2.0	16.7
2)	Her professional activity should be compatible with her family (or community) life	74.9	65.7	44.7	71.7
3)	Her professional activity should be secondary to her family life	15.0	3.4	35.2	7.8
4)	Her activity is to devote herself entirely to her family	1.9	0.0	7.5	0.3
5)	No answer	3.9	17.4	10.6	3.5

Note: Rates in percent.
Chi-square a) = 56.560, significant at the 0.0001 level.
Chi-square b) = 32.006, significant at the 0.0001 level.

One wonders whether the latter might not sometimes explain the former. Table 7.9, reproduced for illustrative purposes, reflects these known differences in an exemplary way, notably the attraction women have for the social interests. The difference between the sexes here is about one standard deviation. An attraction of this kind could give rise to modalities of self-realization that do not rely on occupation alone.

Table 7.10 moves beyond interests to the variables that have to do with a more important and explicit commitment, that is, *predominant plans and effective occupational realizations*. Here again the differences are very marked and practically for the same "dimensions," which this time take the form of occupational categories. In addition, the women's occupational aspirations and realizations are sometimes located on a level inferior to those of the men (cf. the choice of "paramedical" and "social" categories which do not require studies at the university).

In our opinion, *explicit plans* warrant special attention.

Indeed, most adolescents find themselves confronted with having to answer direct questions about their future plans asked by their parents, teachers, friends, etc. It can by hypothesized that formulating plans allows the individual to situate himself or even define himself, by affirming an identity that has yet to be realized but that his circle of relations would like him to outline. Statements made in this context appear far from naive in that adolescents have to adjust them in relation to the reactions of approval, indifference or disapproval that greet them. [Dupont and Jobin, 1987]

In addition, we agree with Gendre in thinking that such plans very probably

Table 7.9
Gender Differences in Occupational Interests Based on Holland's Personal Inventory

	Boys in Latin stream (N=138)	Boys in Science stream (N=152)	Girls in Latin stream (N=135)
	M	**M**	**F**
Holland's scales			
Realistic (mechanics, outdoors)	51.2	54.5	45.4
Investigative (scientific)	48.5	56.7	44.2
Artistic (visual arts, music, literature)	50.8	47.6	51.7
Social (social service, education)	46.4	45.7	56.4
Entrepreneurial (sales, politics, etc.)	51.5	48.0	50.0
Conventional (office, accounting, etc.)	50.8	52.4	47.2

*Average profiles in T scores (M = 50, F = 10) of three groups of subjects extracted from Panel 1 (1975).

Table 7.10
Distribution of Predominant Plans (1974) and Realizations (1982) (Panel 1)

Occupational category	Predominant plan in 1974		Realization in 1982	
	M	F	M	F
Artistic (fine arts)	4.2	8.0	4.5	4.8
Engineer	16.0	1.4	12.5	1.1
Medical	11.4	17.4	14.0	12.2
Paramedical	0.0	12.7	3.0	13.8
Scientific	20.6	7.0	14.7	3.2
Arts	14.4	23.9	10.6	12.7
Law, political science	6.2	2.8	9.1	8.5
Business school (economics)	2.3	0.9	7.2	2.1
Social sciences	2.6	4.2	4.2	9.5
Social service	1.0	15.0	4.2	13.2
Other occupations	11.4	2.8	9.8	10.1
Unknown	9.5	3.8	6.4	9.0
	100.0	100.0	100.0	100.0
	(N=306)	(N=213)	(N=265)	(N=189)

Note: Rates in percent
Chi-square in 1974 = 152.585, significant at the 0.0001 level.
Chi-square in 1982 = 74.15, significant at the 0.0001 level.

correspond to the best overall evaluation that the individual can make of his aspirations, by adjusting the image he has of himself with the image he has of the world of work.

As a means of determining the formulation of future plans (Panel 1), we had at our disposal answers to three specific questions each time information was gathered. We retained either the predominant plan (the one that was expressed the most intensively), or the totality of all the recorded answers, weighted in relation to their intensity. The answers were "reduced" to a number of categories (those figuring in Table 7.10), while the categories selected were those that were best adapted to our data in terms of both plans and subsequent realizations.

Since there were slight fluctuations in the distribution of the answers recorded on three occasions (1974, 1975, 1976) prior the moment of decision, we have reproduced only the first distribution (1974), obtained on the basis of plans formulated by 16- to 17-year-olds, two years before their diploma. This distribution can be compared to that of realizations recorded at the end of the survey (1982), 8 years later, when the subjects were 24 to 25 years old (Table 7.10).

If the plans express a self-image, and the effective choice reflects the realization of such a self-image, there must be a strong correlation between plan(s) and realization(s). In order to evaluate this correlation, we have calculated the *rate of adequacy between predominant plan and effective realization* (Table 7.11), adequacy being defined as maintaining the same occupational category from the moment of making the plan to the moment of its realization. Along with an obvious erosion of validity in proportion to the amount of time between the two, there are also noticeable differences in relation to the moment the plans were formulated. Plans made in 1976, a few weeks before the diploma examinations, turn out to be much more valid than those made previously: 6 years after leaving secondary school, about half the subjects (47%) still fit into the *occupational category* of their former predominant plan.

If Table 7.11 expresses, in any case, a form of self-realization (fidelity to a stable self-image), it is possible that some of the subjects who did change category did so because their self-image had changed. This would also constitute a form of self-realization. Although we did not question the subjects on this point, we did notice that in the three follow-ups (1977, 1979, 1982) the number of subjects who were satisfied with their situation was always considerably higher than the rate of "adequate" subjects.

Plans are a privileged expression of self-image applied to vocational choice, but they constitute only one of the possible modalities of self-image. Other variables of the survey also reflect self-image to various degrees: the list of occupations, Holland's inventory, the list of occupational values, self-assessment of aptitudes, main academic interest, the Adjective Check List. We have no relevant criteria that would allow us to weigh the proportion of self-image pointed up by each of the above instruments, but it is still possible to have a vague idea of them from the brief definitions given in Table 7.1.

That being the case, we have assessed the overall validity of the instruments on the basis of data extracted from a discriminating analysis of the three series of information gathering and the respondents' situations in 1979, that is, in the middle run, three years after they had left the secondary school system. The percentages of correctly predicted situations can be found in Table 7.12.

Table 7.12 first indicates clearly how valid the plans were, plans having been expressed in the same categories as real choices. In addition, we should stress again that stating a plan corresponds to the expression of a behavior that is probably more elaborate than those implied by other variables. The table also suggests a hierarchy of variables. As validity appears in relation to the degree of resemblance existing between the variables and the real choice, the hierarchy begins with plans, descending to interests, occupational values, etc. (reflections of self-image), and ending with marks in school and father's occupation (objective data).[9]

Table 7.11
Rate of Adequacy between the Predominant Occupational Plan and its Effective Realization, Overall Results (Panel 1)

Year (and moment) of the predominant plan	Year (and moment) of its effective realization after the diploma ("bac") (1976)		
	1977	1979	1982
	(1yr.) (2 yrs.) (3 yrs.)	(3 yrs.) (4 yrs.) (5 yrs.)	(6 yrs.) (7 yrs.) (8 yrs.)
1974	37%	36%	31%
1975	42%	40%	35%
1976	63%*	57%	47%
	100% = 500	100% = 504	100% = 454

*Out of a total of 500 subjects, 316 (63%) were declared "adequate." This means that a plan they formulated in 1976 was identical to the 1977 realization, i.e., that it belonged to the same occupational category (artistic, scientific, medical, legal, etc.) as the one realized.

Table 7.12
Assessment of Validity

Assessment of the Overall Validity of a Series of Instruments and Variables Based on Data Extracted from a Discriminant Analysis (Panel 1) (N = 519), Based on Dupont (1983)

Percentage of the effective choices that were correctly predicted (situation in 1979, that is, insertion in one of the 12 occupational "categories" considered: sciences, medecine, arts, law, etc.*), collected from three sets of information gathered before the diploma (baccalauréat) (1974, 1975, 1976).

. list of occupations (6 first scales)	41.3%	o
. list of occupations (5 last scales)	25.8%	
. Holland's inventory (6 scales)	34.2%	o
. list of leisure activities (7 factorial scores)	32.6%	o
. list of occupational values (5 factorial scores)	30.0%	o
. self-assessment of aptitudes (5 factorial scores)	28.4%	o
. main academic interest (1 score)	26.7%	o
. Adjective Check List, ACL (5 scales)	19.0%	o
. marks received for the diploma (3 marks)	13.7%	
. father's occupation	11.2%	

Degree of Correspondence Between the Dominant Plan in 1974, 1975, 1976 and the Effective Realization (Situation in 1979)

predominant plan :

1974	36%
1975	40%
1976	57%

*The complete list of categories can be found in Table 7.1.
°These instruments reflect various aspects of self-image.

It can be observed that the validity of the grouped variables involving self-image is excellent. Despite the clarity of these results, it was necessary to confirm them in the same study by using the 1982 follow-up (1982) and the data relating to Panel 2.

Although the results reported up to this point furnish us with an overall appraisal of the validity of the predictors, they do not indicate the *validity of these same predictors considered on the occupational categories scale*. A recent study (Dupont, Ballif, and Jobin, 1987) has revealed that there exist significant differences among occupational categories, some categories being easier to predict than others. It seems useful to present an example here, culled from a few elements of this study. Among the available variants (Panel 1), we have chosen the one that includes the widest chronological spread, that is, data relating to predictors collected in 1974 and data relating to the occupational situation in 1982, eight years later. We have assessed the validity by calculating the degree of adequacy or the correspondence between predictors and a criterion, such as:

- between the predomiant plan (P) and the 1982 situation;
- between "interests" (I)—that is, the list of occupations, Holland's inventory, leisure activities, and academic interests—and the 1982 situation;
- between a composite set (plans and "interests") and the 1982 situation;
- between a composite set of all the variables (from Table 7.12) and the 1982 situation.

Table 7.13 reproduces the "adequacy rates" and the type of calculation used.

The differences observed, it should be emphasized, are virtually confirmed by the results obtained on 8 other variants from Panel 1 [i.e., the tables showing correspondences between the predictors from 1974, 1975, and 1976, and the follow-up from 1977, 1979, and 1982, or 9 variants (3×3), less the variant from Table 7.13]. The differences are thus relatively stable, although they need to be cross-validated on the level of Panel 2.

Of the numerous remarks that an attentive reading of Table 7.13 might suggest, we will limit ourselves here to two aspects:

- although the composite sets are on the average slightly more valid than homogeneous predictors, the latter can be more valid for one or another particular occupational category;
- certain categories turn out on the average to be better predicted than others.

This being the case, it can be deduced that the constellation of relevant variables varies in relation to occupational categories. In other words, there exists no pattern of definite factors that can be applied uniformly to different situations, that is, no single modality of self-image (for most of the variables used reflect self-image) that can lead to different occupational self-realizations. In terms of diagnostics and prognostics, this interpretation, as it is evoked in the study mentioned above, suggests that we should develop a two-stage strategy; the first approach would be broad in terms of variables and applicable to all the respondents; then, the second approach, having taken individual results into account, would aim at defining more sharply the roles of sex and occupational categores. In both cases, the variables would need to reflect self-image amply.

CONCLUDING REMARKS

From the above results, it can be inferred that academically privileged subjects living in a country with a strong economy tend on the whole to actualize a certain self-image through their occupational choice.

This seems all the more interesting in that the tendency is observed here in the context of a study that had not originally been conceived as a means of verifying this single hypothesis specifically, but of considering it among other hypotheses. However, we still do not know to what extent or how each variable reflects self-image, so we must refer back to the remarks made by Royce and Powell on the problems of operationalizing these concepts. Even if other methods of treatment, such as complex adequacy (Dupont, Ballif, & Jobin, 1987), lead to results that are slightly different to those presented here, the nature and structure of the variables—that is, the instruments— would in no way be affected. The question thus remains open in this respect.

Table 7.13

Assessment of Long-Term Validity (Panel 1): Degree of Correspondence Among Various Predictors (1974) and the Effective Realization (Situation in 1982)

	PREDICTORS				
Occupational category	Plan(P)	Interests(I)	P + I	Total set	R
- Artistic (fine arts)	.38*	.36	.41	.50	21
- Engineering	.46	.57	.53	.57	35
- Medical	.43	.31	.44	.43	60
- Paramedical	.29	.19	.31	.28	34
- Scientific	.36	.31	.43	.49	45
- Arts	.54	.24	.44	.38	52
- Law, political science	.28	.51	.49	.47	40
- Business school (economics)	.13	.19	.26	.30	23
- Social sciences	.17	.08	.27	.23	29
- Social services	.28	.26	.32	.32	36
- Other occupations	.16	.18	.16	.16	45

"Plan" column: Ratio between the number of subjects whose 1974 dominant plan corresponds to the 1982 realization and the number of 1982 realizations.

"Interests" column: Ratio between the number of subjects whose highest score for the totality of interests corresponds to their 1982 category of realization and the number of 1982 realizations.

"P + I" column: Ratio between the number of subjects whose highest score for the totality of interests and plans corresponds to the 1982 category of realization and the number of 1982 realizations.

"Total set" column: Ratio between the number of subjects whose highest score for the total set of variables corresponds to the 1982 category of realization and the number of 1982 realizations.

"R" column: The number of effective realizations for every category in 1982.

*Example: In this case (0.38), of the 21 subjects who have opted for artistic training or occupation in 1982, 8 had "artistic" plans in 1974 (and 13 another type of plan). Therefore the 8/21 ratio gives 0.38.

Although the tendency to self-realization through occupation is considerable, we can ask whether it really concerns all the subjects. On the eve of their diploma or moment of decision-making, 80% of the subjects (Panel 1 and Panel 2) affirm that they are envisaging a particular occupation. Actual self-realization implies adequacy between plans and effective choice. The highest rate of correspondence recorded during follow-up (Panel 1) is 63%. Thus in these two cases the rate of those who are "left out" is not negligible. They consist of subjects who had a given plan but failed to realize it, and subjects who did not have a given plan but who can be found later in the corresponding occupational category. In addition, if the plans formulated in 1976 immediately prior to decision-making turn out to be more valid than the plans made earlier, it means that there is a certain erosion over time, that there are changes and readjustments. Is it not possible that these readjustments are made as a result of the discovery of self-image on the one hand, and of adaptations to new circumstances on the other? Yet the proportion of these two types of subjects cannot be easily determined. In the study cited above, we mention the fact that the satisfaction rate of the respondents is higher than the adequacy rate. Does this mean that "happiness" is more frequently perceived than self-realization? The answer is uncertain in the sense that "adequate" subjects are slightly more often satisfied than the other subjects.

At the same time, a certain "shift" during the interval between plans and realization can be observed. In certain occupational categories (business school and economics, social sciences, etc.) there are more realizations than plans.

Although our subjects' situation is in principle a more privileged one, the adequacy rates for plans and choice (Table 7.11) are comparable to those found by Noeth and Jepsen (1981) operating on data extracted "from a national sample of high school juniors."[10] Moreover, the occupational interests of our subjects toward the fields chosen are very close to those of other groups or samples of subjects mentioned in relevant literature. It is true, of course, that our European and American colleagues, like ourselves, have dealt with more or less privileged subjects—that is, those who continue with higher education.

Our subjects may have reactions similar to those found in other comparable populations, but the case would undoubtedly be different for groups with lower scholastic achievement and those living in less favored socioeconomic regions. It is probable that in these cases the subjective factors or aspects would be less strongly affirmed,[11] that the volume and breadth of the job market would limit tendencies toward self-realization through this channel, or that in milieus where work and self are not dominant values, other modes of adaptation to life would appear. In the more or less long term, it is possible that women's reactions would differ from men's, and in a more marked way, in more disadvantaged milieus.

RECOMMENDATIONS

Finally, we feel that it would be useful to go beyond the above conclusions and make a few recommendations from various angles.

One cannot deny the interest and usefulness of programs devoted during the school years to preparing students and raising their awareness about vocational choice. But we think that there should be more active intervention when the subjects perceive the moment of decision-making as being near at hand in their own temporal perspective, a perspective that is much shorter than that of adults.

In any preparation program it is absolutely necessary to include a precise individualized follow-through of the subjects. Programs like SDS (Self-Directed Search) seem inadequate for many subjects, especially for (academically, ethnically, etc.) disadvantaged subjects. In order to really measure personal characteristics (locate and interpret information about the self) and apply them adequately (apply knowledge about self to career opportunities) a counselor has to be available to act both as enlightener and as moderator. Self-assessment of aptitudes, for example, is entirely inadequate. [On this issue see the recent study by Lowman and Williams (1987).] At the end of the operations, concrete help in making the decision should be provided, using procedures such as those developed by Cochran (1983), for example.

As regards taking self-image into consideration, it is certainly worth while to apply procedures of the WAY type, in conjunction with other classic approaches. All of them can be placed in a synthetic theoretical framework like the one proposed by Royce and Powell—even if this framework, which is still provisional, requires adjustments to make it useable in the context of vocational guidance.

At the same time, there is still more to be done on the more scientific level of applied research. We believe it would be useful to carry out new surveys which are more closely linked than ours to the dynamics of self-realization. It is especially important to make surveys of male and female adult populations. These populations differ from adolescents not only because of their personal characteristics, but also because of the specific problems they encounter when changing jobs or returning to work. Operations of this sort would concern persons on whom personal history and previous work have already left their mark.

NOTES

1. It could be worth while to compile an inventory of recent studies on the subject and thereby extend Osipow's general survey and assessments (Osipow, 1983).

2. Guilford's and Cattell's factorial models come to mind here.

3. Those of Mulford and Salisbury, for instance.

4. Some additional information can be found in a recent text by Osipow (1987).

5. Panel 1 corresponds to a representative sample (306 boys, 213 girls) of students from the classical, scientific and modern language streams in French-speaking Switzerland; Panel 2 is a sample that is approximately representative of the same population (85 boys, 112 girls).

6. These do not appear on Table 7.4.

7. The differences observed between men and women in Panel 1 do not appear in Panel 2. We thus hesitate to take them into account.

8. In 1975, 75% of the girls thought that a woman's professional activity should be compatible with her family life and only 15% thought it should be secondary. In response to this same question, 45% of the boys were in favor of compatibility and 35% gave priority to the family. It should be noted that other European studies reveal a similar difference between male and female adolescents on the subject of the role of women (de Singly, 1987).

9. As for school marks, which we recorded only for 1976, it should be remembered that they constitute only a sample of performances limited to the marks the three streams had in common (Table 7.1). As for the father's occupation, the very slight validity is due to the fact that only 40% of the fathers had attended university, whereas 80% of the children in these privileged academic categories aspire to higher education and a slightly smaller percentage actually enter university. Operating in another context, Seifert has recently shown (Seifert et al., 1987) that the validity of these objective data is lower than that of variables that reflect self-image.

10. "Expressed vocational choices correctly predicted actual occupations 2 years after high school for 38% of the total sample. Hit rates for males and females were 40% and 35%, respectively."

11. And there would be greater attention to other factors (job security, for example).

REFERENCES

Allport, G. 1955. *Becoming*. New Haven: Yale University Press.

Ballif, J.-F. 1980. Etude factorielle et longitudinale de l'échelle de maturité des attitudes vocationelles de Crites. *Révue Suisse de psychologie pure et appliquées*, 39, 310–329.

Berthoud, S. 1983. *Les intérêts des candidats bacheliers*. Lausanne: Faculté des Sciences sociales et politiques de l'Université.

Borkowsky, A., Kaestli, E., Ley, K., and Streckeisen, U. 1985. *Zwei Welten. Ein Leben*. Zürich: Unionsverlag.

Burns, R. B. 1979. *The Self Concept*. London/New York: Longman.

Cochran, L. 1983. Seven measures of the ways that deciders frame their career decisions. *Measurement and Evaluation in Guidance*, 16(3): 67–77.

de Singly, F. 1987. *Fortune et infortune de la femme mariée*. Paris: Presses Universitaires de France.

Diggory, J. C., and Magaziner, D. E. 1959. L'auto-évaluation en fonction de capacités utiles en vue de buts particuliers. *Bulletin de l'Association internationale de psychologie appliquée.*, 8(1): 46–63.

Dupont, J.-B. 1979. *Inventaire personnel de J. L. Holland* [Manual]. Issy-les-Moulineaux: Establissements d'applications psychotechniques.

Dupont, J.-B. 1983. A propos de la genèse du choix professionnel chez les futurs bacheliers. In *Les lycéens face à l'enseignement supérieur.* Issy-les-Moulineaux: Establissements d'applications psychotechniques, pp. 55–71.

Dupont, J.-B., Ballif, J.-F., and Jobin, C. 1987. Rôle et fonction des intérêts dans la définition du projet professionnel. *L'orientation scolaire et professionnelle,* 16: 207–229.

Dupont, J.-B., and Jobin, C. 1987. Projets explicites et genèse du choix professionnel, *7èmes journées de psychologie différentielle.* Nancy: Université 2, pp. 24–25.

Dupont, J.-B., Leresche, G., Ballif, J.-F., Descombes, J.-P., and Muller, M. A. 1981–1982. Définition et mesure des valeurs professionnelles chez les futurs bacheliers. *Bulletin de Psychologie,* 35: 449–471.

Gendre, F., and Ogay, C. 1973. L'évaluation de la personnalité à l'aide de l'Adjective Check List (ACL) de H. Gough. *Révue suisse de psychologie,* 32: 332–347.

Ghiselli, E. E. 1954. The forced-choice technique in self description. *Personnel Psychology,* 7: 201–208.

Lavoegie, M. S. 1958. Note sur une épreuve d'auto-définition. *Le Travail Humain,* 21(3–4): 325–332.

L'Ecuyer, R. 1978. *Le concept de soi.* Paris: Presses Universitaires de France.

Loevinger, J. 1978. *Scientific Ways in the Study of Ego Development.* Worcester, Mass.: Glack University Press.

Lowman, R. L., and Williams, R. E. 1987. Validity of self-ratings of abilities and competences. *Journal of Vocational Behavior,* 31(1): 1–13.

Mabe, P. A., and West, S. G. 1982. Validity of self-evaluation of ability: A review and meta-analysis. *Journal of Applied Psychology,* 67(3): 280–296.

Markus, H., and Wurf, E. 1987. The dynamic self-concept: A social psychological perspective. *Annual Review of Psychology,* 38: 299–338.

Noeth, R. J., and Jepsen, D. A. 1981. Predicting field of job entry from expressed vocational choice and certainty level. *Journal of Counseling Psychology,* 28(1): 22–26.

Osipow, S. H. 1983. *Theories of Career Development,* 3rd ed. Englewood Cliffs, N.J.: Prentice-Hall.

Osipow, S. H. 1987. Counseling psychology: Theory, research, and practice in career counseling. *Annual Review of Psychology,* 38: 257–278.

Perloff, R. 1987. Self-interest and personal responsibility redux. *American Psychologist,* 42(1): 3–11.

Rey, A. 1958. Evaluation par l'individu de quelques attributs de sa propre personne. *Révue suisse de psychologie pure et appliquée,* 17(1): 40–47.

Rosenberg, M. 1957. *Occupations and Values.* Glencoe, Ill.: Free Press.

Royce, J. R., and Powell, A. 1983. *Theory of Personality and Individual Differences: Factors, Systems, and Processes.* Englewood Cliffs, N.J.: Prentice-Hall.

Seifert, K. H., Bergmann, C., and Eder, F. 1987. Berufswahlreife und Selbstkonzept-Berufkonzept-Kongruenz als Prädiktoren der beruflichen Anpassung und Bewährung während der beruflichen Ausbildung. *Zeit. für Arbeits-und Organisationspsychologie, 31*(4): 133–143.

8

Self-Realization
in Modern Women

Nancy E. Betz

The position taken in this chapter is that self-realization, along with psychological adjustment and overall life satisfaction, are most effectively achieved, for women as well as for men, through involvement in a constellation of life-career roles" (Super, 1980) emphasizing "work-related positions and roles along with coordinate avocational, familial, and civic roles (Super, 1980, p. 282). Given this position, it is further suggested that *overemphasis* on women's traditional roles of wife and mother and concomitant *deemphasis* on their career pursuits have had serious negative effects on their self-realization and their psychological adjustment and well-being. However, current societal changes leading to fuller and more satisfying labor force participation and to involvement in a wider variety of life roles are facilitating positive change in women's lives, toward greater self-realization and psychological adjustment and well-being.

In the following discussion, research is reviewed which suggests the beneficial effects of broadened roles on women's self-realization and, conversely, some of the negative effects of the narrower traditional roles. The discussion begins with an overview of the assumptions on which these ideas are based. Second, barriers to women's self-realization are discussed, beginning with the serious problem of the underutilization of female intellectual potential and proceeding to discussion of the negative effects of a sole focus on the homemaking role on women's adjustment and self-esteem. The chapter ends with suggestions for means of addressing the current barriers to full self-realization among women, including approaches to the management of multiple roles, possible educational and counseling interventions, and recommendations for needed theory and research.

BASIC ASSUMPTIONS

Any application of a concept as broad as self-realization to the lives of women in society requires one to make certain assumptions. For the present chapter, several major assumptions, largely based on research findings, were made.

The first assumption concerning self-realization in modern women is that women, like men, need a variety of major sources of satisfaction in their lives—as once stated by Freud (according to Erik Erikson, 1950), the psychologically well-adjusted human being is able "to love and to work" effectively. Both men and women need the satisfactions of interpersonal relationships, with family and/or friends, but also the satisfaction of achievement in the outside world. Osipow (1983), in his major treatise on theories of career development, states that: "It is clear that working holds an important place both in society and in the lives of individuals" (p. vii). And as stated by Baruch and Barnett (1980, p. 244):

It is almost a cliche now for people who work long hours at demanding jobs, aware of what they are missing in terms of time with family, long talks with friends, concerts, all kinds of oportunities for leisure, to express the sentiment that "there is more to life than work." The problem is that life *without* productive work is terrible. We assume this for men in thinking about their unemployment and retirement, but we do not think about the situation of women in this way.

As is implied in the above statement, neither men nor women have had the opportunity to lead truly balanced lives; the careers of many men have caused them to miss important interpersonal satisfactions (Gilbert and Rachlin, 1987), and, conversely, the home and family responsibilities of women have often led to sacrifice in their career lives (Betz and Fitzgerald, 1987; Gilbert and Rachlin, 1987). Research on adult development (Fiske and Weiss, 1977; Lowenthal, Thurnher, and Chiriboga, 1975) indicates that, in midlife, the regrets of women focus around their lack of outward accomplishment and fulfillment of potential while the regrets of men focus on their lack of feeling of connectedness with their families. Men tend to turn toward the family in middle age, while women yearn for the external world. Since this chapter is about women, its focus is on the imbalance in women's lives but that in the lives of men is no less important as an issue of self-realization and psychological adjustment.

A second major assumption, fully elaborated in the next section, is that self-realization requires the fulfillment of individual potential for achievement. Although the roles of homemaker and mother are vitally important and often very satisfying, they do not allow most women to fulfill their unique abilities and talents. These, rather, must be fulfilled through career pursuits or volunteer and avocational activities, just as they are in men. This is not to discount the importance of childrearing but only its *insufficiency* as a life-long answer to the issue of self-realization. Even if a woman spends a number of years creatively rearing children, these children inevitably grow up and begin their own lives, lives that must of necessity be increasingly independent from the parental home. Super (1980; also Nevill and Super, 1986) emphasize the *dynamic* nature of role involvement—important life roles wax and wane over the life span, and there is no reason to expect that *one* role can fulfill one's needs either at a given point in time or over time.

As will be reviewed in the next section, the evidence is very strong that homemakers who do not have other outlets for achievement and productivity are highly susceptible to psychological distress, particularly as children grow and leave home. Thus, women who have not dealt with issues of self-realization earlier in life will be faced with that task in mid-life, whether or not they are prepared.

In essence, I argue herein that the major means for self-realization—that is, productive work, the opportunity for creativity and achievement, and the actualization of one's individual potentialities—are essentially the same for women and men, but that the societal roles of women have reduced their access to these means of self-realization. Certainly interpersonal relationships, including those with spouse and children, bring many people great satisfaction, but the term *"self-realization"* implies an individual focus, a self-exploration and self-development that must prioritize at least to some extent *oneself* versus the needs of others. In the next sections, evidence for the negative effects of exclusive emphasis on traditional roles for women's self-realization will be reviewed. Following that, the advantages of career and multiple role involvement for women's self-realization will be discussed.

SELF-REALIZATION AND WOMEN'S ROLES

Concepts of self-realization or self-actualization, for example those of Edgar Krau in this volume and Abraham Maslow in such works as *Motivation and Personality* (1954), emphasize the importance of realizing and fulfilling one's individual potential. Even an ordinary dictionary recognizes the central component of self-realization; for example, the 1982 edition of the *American Heritage Dictionary* defines self-realization as "The complete development or fulfillment of one's own potential" and defines the term "to self-actualize" as "To achieve one's full potential."

In traditional psychology, the concept of individual potential has referred to characteristics such as talents, intelligence, abilities, interests, values, and personality traits (see major texts on individual differences, especially Anastasi, 1965; Tyler, 1965, 1978; see also Betz, Fitzgerald, and Hill, 1989). Most usually these major individual differences are thought to be actualized through work-related or career pursuits and/or creative endeavors, and secondarily through avocational (leisure) pursuits. Frank Parsons, in his 1909 book *Choosing a Vocation*, introduced this idea to vocational psychology with his "matching model" of career choice—stating that optimal career choices are those that fit the individual's talents, abilities, and interests. Super (1957) postulated that individuals form a self-concept which, in the optimal case, is used to select a career having a similar "vocational self-concept." And Crites (1978), in his theory of career maturity, suggests that the realism of a career choice—that is, the fit between the individual's abilities and interests and the level and field of the occupation selected—is a sine qua non of career maturity versus immaturity.

Examples of individuals whose work allowed them to fulfill at least some of their intellectual and creative potentialities include Anne Roe's biologists (1951a), physical scientists (1951b), and psychologists and anthropologists (1953). These successful scientists were generally happily immersed in their scientific work throughout life. Studies of artists (Barron and Welsh, 1952; Eiduson, 1958), musicians (Seashore, 1939), and architects, mathematicians, poets, and writers (MacKinnon, 1962) offer further examples of people who have loved their work and made lasting contributions to society. Gifted athletes, physicians, craftworkers, and engineers also provide examples of people who develop and utilize their individual talents and abilities through their work.

Although not everyone has a truly special gift or driving life interest, the existence of both genetically and environmentally determined individual differences in major psychological attributes suggests the wisdom of Parsons' (1909) initial model, that is, the idea that life decisions will maximize self-realization when they involve a fit or congruence between the individual and the career chosen. Unfortunately, the choice of the role of homemaker and mother may fulfill a *societally approved* role for women, but it is inadequate as a means of actualizing the vast individual differences *among* women. More specifically, the traditional roles of women have resulted in a tremendous underutilization of female abilities and talents, an underutilization which has had significant costs for society as well as for the self-realization of women themselves.

Barrier to Individual Self-Realization: The Underutilization of Female Ability

In contrast to men, women's intellectual capacities and talents have not been reflected in their educational and occupational achievements. Even for women who have elected to work outside the home rather than focusing on the roles of homemaker and mother, their career aspirations and choices have been far lower in level than are the aspirations of males with comparable levels of ability (Fitzgerald and Crites, 1980).

One general principle of vocational psychology posits a relationship between intellect and achievement such that more intelligent people are expected to achieve more, first educationally and then occupationally (Crites, 1969; Tyler, 1965). Among men, the relationship of intellect to obtained educational and occupational levels holds reasonably well (Tyler, 1978). Among women, however, the relationship begins to break down in adolescence, and by college age and beyond it has broken down almost completely for the majority of women. Women fail to use their talents and abilities in educational and career pursuits, resulting in losses both to themselves and to societies that need their talents.

Ironically, females start out as the higher achievers in comparison to males and as the children more likely to utilize their abilities in educational pursuits. Girls perform better academically than boys at all educational levels. Studies going back as far as 1929 have shown that girls obtain higher school grades than do boys, beginning in elementary school and continuing through college (Carnegie Commission on Higher Education, 1973; Hyde, 1985; Tyler, 1965). Among 1960 Project Talent seniors, 51 percent of the girls in comparison to 39 percent of the boys reported high school averages of mostly As and Bs (Carnegie Commission on Higher Education, 1973).

The school progress of girls is also superior to that of boys. Girls less frequently need to repeat a grade, and girls are more likely than boys to be accelerated and promoted (cf. Hyde, 1985). In college, women consistently receive higher grades than do men in major fields ranging from the humanities and social sciences to the sciences, engineering, and even mathematics. Women's grade-point advantage ranges between one-half and one full grade point, depending on the major field. Even so, the higher we go in educational systems, the greater the dropout rate among women, usually for non-academic reasons. Thus, many more men than women earn graduate and professional degrees, even when women were initially performing as well or better academically.

Women's underutilization of their abilities is even more apparent in the occupational realm. Assuming few or no major gender differences in vocationally relevant abilities (see major reviews by Betz and Fitzgerald, 1987; Hyde, 1981; Maccoby and Jacklin, 1974), we would assume an approximately equal tendency of women as of men to achieve high occupational levels and to achieve eminence. Unfortunately, this has not been the case, with only negligible representation of women among the eminent throughout history. For example, fewer than 10% of the people who could be characterized as eminent based on having entries in standard biographical dictionaries have been women, and more than half of those women were listed because they were sovereigns and were thus eminent by birth or were the wives or mistresses of famous men (Anastasi, 1965).

An early attempt to study eminence in women (Castle, 1913) found only 868 eminent women across 42 nations and extending from the seventh century BC. The largest number of these had achieved eminence in literature, but the highest *level* of eminence (as indicated by the number of lines allocated in the biographical dictionary) was achieved by sovereigns, political leaders, and mothers or mistresses of eminent men. Other non-intellectual ways in which women achieved eminence (or at least the fame necessary to be listed in a biographical dictionary) was through great beauty, a tragic fate, or being immortalized in literature (Castle, 1913).

Among the women who would have been likely to achieve eminence had they been born male were the gifted girls in the longitudinal studies of gifted children of Lewis Terman, Maud Merrill, and Robert Oden at Stanford University in the United States. The gifted children, originally studied in 1921–1922, consisted of 1,528 children having measured IQs equal to or greater than 135. Of the sample, 671 were girls and 847 were boys. When followed up at midlife (Terman and Oden, 1959), the vast majority of men had achieved considerable prominence in scientific, creative, professional, and managerial realms. As a group they had, by their mid-40s, been exceptionally productive scientists, made exceptional literary and artistic contributions, and become prominent in a variety of fields.

In contrast to the men, the women were primarily housewives or were employed in fields traditionally dominated by women. About 50% of the gifted women were housewives. Of those who were working full-time, 21 percent were teachers in elementary or secondary schools, 8 percent were social workers, 20 percent were secretaries, and 8 percent were librarians or nurses. Two-thirds of the women with IQs equal to or greater than 170 (clearly genius level) were housewives or office workers. Only very small proportions were physicians, lawyers, psychologists, academicians, executives, or musicians. Although the girls had been judged most artistically gifted as children, and the seven most talented writers in the original group were girls, as adults *all* the artists and writers were men (Terman and Oden, 1959). As children these women had been as intellectually gifted as their male counterparts, but their achievements in adulthood were clearly in contrast to their early intellectual promise. Their sex, not their individual potential, was the best predictor of their occupational accomplishments in adulthood.

Thus, ability and talent in gifted girls had almost no relationship to their achievements as women. At least seven talented writers, as well as unknown numbers of artists, musicians, biologists, geneticists, and astronomers, were lost to the world. As stated in the report of the Carnegie Commission on Higher Education (1973), "The supply of human intelligence is limited, and the demand for it in society is even greater. The largest unused supply is found among women" (p. 27). Even more importantly for this chapter, however, is the loss of opportunities among women themselves for individual self-actualization and fulfillment of potential.

Bem and Bem (1976) have described the phenomenon illustrated by the Terman studies as indicative of the "homogenization of women." In other words, women are socialized to pursue the same roles (those of wife and mother or, if employed, a traditionally female career) *regardless* of their individual capabilities and talents. A woman's accomplishments can often be predicted on the basis of her sex, literally without any other information about her. It would be as if the parents of all baby boys were told that their sons would be factory workers when they were adults, regardless of the unique talents and abilities of each boy. Although this restriction in choice may be characteristic of some totalitarian states, we have come to expect more freedom and opportunity for self-realization in industrialized democracies.

The dramatic underutilization of female talent demonstrated by the Terman study has been replicated consistently in more recent research. For example, Card, Steel, and Abeles (1980) reported the results of a long-term follow-up of the ninth-grade cohort of the original Project Talent study. Project Talent, conducted by researchers at the University of Pittsburgh (Flanagan, 1971), was a large-scale longitudinal study of 440,000 ninth-through twelfth-graders carefully sampled from 1,353 secondary schools across the United States. Students were originally administered a battery of tests in 1960. Follow-up surveys measuring subjects' educational and occupational attainment 1, 5, and 11 years after subjects' expected high school graduation were also conducted.

Card et al. reported that while the female students had had higher high school grades and scored higher on a composite of academic ability tests, by 11 years after high school the men had obtained significantly more education and were earning significantly more money. Sex differences in realization of potential were found across all SES levels, and differences widened from the 5-year to the 11-year follow-up. The widening of the achievement gap was most apparent for the most talented female students, those in the top quartile as ninth-graders. In other words, by age 29 the brightest men are beginning to manifest their intellectual potential while the bright women fall further and further short of their potential for educational and occupational achievement.

And most recently, in the United States at least, a study of 80 Illinois high school valedictorians showed that even those girls who had graduated from high school at the top of their classes were compromising on or giving up their college and employment plans ("Women Cut Aims . . .," 1987). Of the 46 women valedictorians, only 35% were still planning to work full-time six years after high school graduation, in contrast to all of the 34 men valedictorians. And, even more disturbing, while the men's intellectual self-esteem remained stable or increased throughout college, that of the women was lower at the time of the study than when they had finished high school.

In summary, girls surpass boys in school achievement at all levels, but in terms of ultimate educational and occupational *level* achieved, females lag far behind males. Numerous barriers to women's self-realization in careers operate to reduce the extent to which women's abilities, and even their superior performance in school, are actualized in later achievements, not to mention actual eminence.

Barriers to Women's Achievements

Numerous writers have discussed barriers to women's achievements. Among the earliest were Matthews and Tiedeman (1964), who specified four conflicts unique to females: (1) the female's concern that career aspirations and achievements would necessitate the sacrifice of marriage, (2) sex-typed family roles qualifying women for homemaker but not breadwinner roles; (3) home–career conflict; and (4) the concurrence of the desired age of marriage with the need to emphasize educational pursuits and goals necessary to career achievements. Note the theme of these barriers, that is, the difficulty for women of having both a successful marriage and a successful career. Men have never had to choose between these, yet painful choices involving the sacrifice of one or the other have faced women.

Farmer (1976) suggested six internal or self-concept barriers to women, including fear of success, sex role orientation, low risk-taking behavior, home–career conflict, and low academic self-esteem, and three environmental barriers, including discrimination, family socialization, and the lack of availability of resources like child care. Falk and Cosby (1978) mentioned as disruptive to female achievement the sex-typing of occupations, the perceived conflict between marital and occupational success, and the pressure of others toward the traditional female role and away from career-oriented pursuits. Betz and Fitzgerald (1987; see also Fitzgerald and Betz, 1983) review additional barriers, including occupational stereotypes, bias from career counselors toward traditional female roles, and lack of support from counselors, parents, significant others, and friends for innovative, demanding career pursuits. Other theories strongly emphasize the limiting nature of the societal opportunity structure (Astin, 1984) and socioculturally based sex-typed expectations (Gottfredson, 1981; Perun and Bielby, 1981) on the range of choices that women perceive for themselves.

Several points about these barriers in relationship to self-realization should be especially noted. First, they tend to limit rather than to expand options—both in terms of traditional women's roles and traditionally female-dominated careers, women have been limited in their choices. Self-actualization and self-realization, in the view of this author, are most likely to occur in the context of a wide range of options available to the individual; thus, societally based restrictions in the perceived range of options will have a suppressive effect on the potential for self-realization.

Second, these barriers emphasize *external* pressures away from some options and toward others; research reviewed by Betz and Fitzgerald (1987), among others, strongly suggests the importance of such external pressures in the decisions that women make about career pursuits. Unfortunately, self-realization is, by definition, a matter of realizing and fulfilling one's own needs and capabilities; it simply cannot be done optimally if it is done for or in response to others rather than for and in response to one's self.

Even after initial choices have been made, women face further barriers to the career achievements. As is extensively reviewed in Betz and Fitzgerald (1987), women have had more difficulty implementing their choices and more difficulty achieving success and satisfaction after getting started in their careers. Major internal or self-concept barriers to career success and satisfaction include: (1) self-doubt, often caused by taking discrimination personally instead of recognizing it as discrimination; (2) fear of the attitudes of others toward her as a "career woman"; and (3) guilt stemming from her feelings that she is neglecting her family in order to pursue a career.

A major external barrier is multiple-role overload, resulting from the expectations of others that the full-time pursuit of a career should not lessen her sole responsibility for her traditional tasks of homemaker and child-rearer. Although multiple roles have many advantages, to be discussed in a subsequent section, women who for all practical purposes hold two full-time jobs, that is, both a career and the job of homemaker and mother, are required to be twentieth-century "Superwomen" unless they find other ways to cope with the massive demands of their roles. Other external barriers include discrimination in the educational and work worlds, involving inequities in pay, promotions, benefits, the award of fellowships and scholarships, and so forth; tokenism, that is, being the only woman at her level in an organization or department (a lonely and often uncomfortably visible position); and lack of support from others, for example, lack of women mentors and role models and lack of professional or collegial support systems in many environments.

Summary

The serious problem of the underutilization of female potential for self-realization can be addressed, at least in part, by attention to the internal and external barriers faced by women. Internal barriers can be addressed by changes in the socialization of young girls, through improved education and counselling, and through efforts to provide women with role models, mentors, and support for their educational and career aspirations. External barriers can be addressed by societal and organizational change, including legal and legislative progress. The problem of multiple role overload must be addressed by changing views of women's sole responsibility for home and children, so that both women and men may share the responsibilities of a variety of life roles, for example, those of home and children as well as those of "breadwinning" and achieving in career pursuits.

WOMEN, SELF-REALIZATION, AND PSYCHOLOGICAL ADJUSTMENT

In addition to the problem of underutilization of abilities, there is strong evidence that failure to develop one's individual capabilities and interests in career pursuits has negative effects on psychological adjustment and self-esteem. There are three lines of evidence for this point, one coming from the literature on correlates of psychological disturbance, a second from the literature on self-esteem, and the third relating the sex-role–related characteristics of masculinity and femininity to self-esteem and adjustment.

Psychological Disturbance

First, most current literature on mental health and well-being suggests the positive effects of expanded life roles for women and, conversely, the negative effects of the traditional role alone. Beginning with the women in the Terman gifted sample, when followed up in their 60s (Sears and Barbie, 1977), the women who reported the highest levels of life satisfaction were the employed women. Least satisfied with their lives were those who had been housewives all of their adult lives. The most psychologically disturbed women were those with exceptionally high IQs (above 170) who had not worked outside the home. It seems fairly clear that women with genius-level IQs who have not pursued meaningful careers outside the home have been unable to achieve self-realization and have suffered psychological consequences for that failure.

More generally, there is strong evidence for the salutary effects of working outside the home on a woman's psychological adjustment, regardless of her marital status. Bernard, in an analysis (1971) of the relationship between marital status and psychological health, concluded that the healthiest individuals were the married men and the single women, while married women were at particularly high risk for psychological distress. Further analyses of the relationships of marital status to mental health by Gove and Tudor (1973) and Radloff (1975), among others, led to similar conclusions.

However, it does not seem to be marriage per se that is detrimental to women's psychological adjustment, but rather the lack of meaningful paid employment. In the studies mentioned, the women who were *not employed* accounted for the surplus of psychological distress among the married women. Frederic Ilfeld (1977), in a large-scale study of households in the Chicago, Illinois, area, found that the women who were as psychologically healthy and free from symptoms of distress as the average man were those employed in high-prestige occupations. But Ilfeld and also Ferree (1976) found that even working-class employed women were happier and had higher self-esteem than their nonworking counterparts. Bart (1971), in a study of middle-aged women, found that employed women were much less susceptible to menopausal depression than were women who had concentrated all their attention on the home; women who were overidentified and overinvolved with children who had recently left home (leaving the "empty nest") were the most vulnerable to depression in middle age.

It should be noted that aggegrate data on the relationship of mental health to marital and employment status do not describe all individuals; there are undoubtedly some women whose individual characteristics are ideally suited for the activities involved in homemaking and childrearing. Even for women such as these, however, the salience and requirements of the role of homemaker and mother eventually decrease substantially as children grow up and leave home (Hoffman, 1977), and new means for the derivation of a sense of self-worth and self-realization must be sought. Again, Super's (1980) idea of a dynamic constellation of life-career roles is pertinent.

Self-Esteem

The crucial importance of a positive self-concept to psychological health and optimal functioning has long been a fundamental assumption in psychology (e.g., Rogers, 1951). Furthermore, the self-concept plays a central role in at least one theory of career choice and development, that of Donald Super (1957, 1963). Although there is by no means agreement across researchers on the definitions of self-concept, self-esteem, and related terms, whether they are global, unidimensional terms or multi-dimensional concepts, nor on how they should be measured, there *is* agreement on their importance. In the section below, the relationship of global self-esteem to women's employment status is reviewed. For more detailed reviews of the self-concept and self-esteem literatures, see works by Rosenberg (1979), Wells and Marwell (1976), and Wylie (1979).

Measures of global self-esteem, or overall self-evaluation and self-accept-ance, include the self-esteem, self-acceptance, and self-confidence scales from widely used personality inventories such as the California Psychological Inventory (Gough, 1957) and the Sixteen Personality Factor Questionnaire (Cattell, Eber, and Tatsuoka, 1970). Other specially constructed measures include the Rosenberg Self-Esteem Scale (Rosenberg, 1965), the Coopersmith (1967) Self-Esteem Scale, and the Self-Assurance Scale of the Ghiselli (1971) Self-Description Inventory.

Although sex differences on global measures of self-esteem are not consistently found, studies using such measures consistently report more positive self-concepts and higher levels of self-esteem among career-oriented, versus home-oriented, women (e.g. Tinsley and Faunce, 1980). Greater self-confidence and self-esteem have been found to be associated with stronger career orientation among adolescent girls (Baruch, 1976; Ridgeway and Jacobsen, 1979). Self-esteem is strongly related to achievement motivation in both male and female college students, and the relationship appears to be even stronger for female than for male students (Stericker and Johnson, 1977).

High levels of self-esteem are particularly characteristic of women in male-dominated occupations, such as Bachtold's (1976) women scientists, artists, writers, and politicians, Bachtold and Werner's (1970) psychologists, and Lemkau's (1983) physicians and attorneys. Greenhaus and Simon (1976) reported that female students higher in self-esteem showed greater correspondence between their real and their ideal choices than did students lower in self-esteem. Thus, since real–ideal correspondence can be thought to suggest self-actualized behavior, the suggested relationship between career orientation and self-realization receives further empirical support.

Instrumentality, Expressiveness, and Androgyny

Another set of characteristics that has received extensive study in relationship to psychological adjustments, self-esteem, and women's roles is that previously studied as the concepts of "masculinity" and "femininity" and, more recently, as "instrumentality" and "expressiveness".

Beginning in the 1970s, a number of writers (e.g. Bem, 1974; Spence, Helmreich, and Stapp, 1975) suggested that masculinity and femininity were appropriately conceptualized as separate, independent dimensions rather than as opposite ends of a single dimension, as they had been conceptualized in personality inventories such as the Minnesota Multiphasic Personality Inventory (the Mf scale, or Scale 5). With this newer conceptualization, an individual of either sex could possess relatively high levels of both masculinity and femininity, relatively low levels of both, or a high level of one in combination with a low level of the other.

In Bem's (1977) formulation, possession of both masculine and feminine characteristics was postulated to be advantageous because so-called "androgynous" individuals would have maximal behavioral flexibility and adaptability; such individuals would be freer of artificial sex-role–related constraints on the extent of their behavioral and coping repertoires. For example, an androgynous individual would theoretically be able to display adaptive "masculine" behaviors (e.g. assertiveness, active problem-solving) *and* adaptive feminine behaviors (e.g. giving emotional support to others) as appropriate to situational demands. Especially pertinent to the topic of this chapter is the idea that because androgynous individuals would be less constrained by sex roles, they would be more likely to engage in maximally self-actualizing behaviors. For example, the boy with talent as a dancer and the girl with aptitude for carpentry would be more likely to realize those talents if free from sex-role constraints.

Although a large body of research literature has examined these concepts and, generally, supported the validity of the underlying theory (see the extensive review by Cook, 1985), there is an increasing tendency to avoid the terms "masculinity" and "femininity" in favor of terms that better summarize the actual behaviors and characteristics represented (Spence and Helmreich, 1980). Instead of the term "masculinity," the term "instrumentality," which refers to the capabilities of self-assertion and competence, has been suggested by Spence and Helmreich to summarize descriptively the key aspects of traditional masculinity. The term "expressiveness" best summarizes the central aspects of traditional femininity, that is, nurturance, interpersonal concern, and emotional expressiveness and sensitivity. Similarly, David Bakan's (1966) distinction between "agentic" (self-assertive, motivated to master) and "communal" (concerned with others, selfless) characteristics provides an alternative set of descriptive labels for what is measured by masculinity and femininity scales.

Regardless of the labels used to report the results of research in this area, this research has consistently and convincingly shown the importance of these constellations of characteristics, particularly instrumentality or masculinity, to mental health in women and men (Spence et al., 1975). Self-esteem and personal adjustment are uniformly found to be highest in masculine and androgynous individuals of both sexes, with the superiority of androgyny to masculinity varying across studies but always superior to femininity alone in both sexes (Bem, 1977; Gilbert, 1981; Spence et al., 1975). These findings do not suggest that feminine expressiveness is a negative characteristic, but only that the capability of instrumental behavior is vital to adjustment, coping, and self-esteem.

Given the importance of instrumentality to well-being, self-esteem, and psychological adjustment, it is again instructive to note that the characteristic of instrumentality is strongly related to career orientation in women and to both the extent and nature of women's career pursuits. Higher levels of instrumentality are related to stronger career orientation (Abrahams, Feldman, and Nash, 1978; Greenglass and Devins, 1982), to a greater extent of labor force participation following the birth of the first child (Gaddy, Glass, and Arnkoff, 1983), and to a greater career achievement among working women (Wong, Kettlewell, and Sproule, 1985). Orlovsky and Stake (1981) reported that masculinity was related to stronger achievement motivation and to greater self-esteem and self-perceived capabilities among college women.

Most strongly related to instrumentality, however, is pursuit of careers in nontraditional fields for women. Willingness to consider nontraditional majors, or, alternatively stated, less susceptibility to the limiting influences of traditional female socialization, was the major explanation of Wolfe and Betz' (1981) finding that masculine-typed women were more likely than feminine-typed women to prefer careers congruent with their measured vocational interests. Thus, the "matching model" as a basis for career decision-making, and, thus, greater actualization of "self" in adult pursuits, may be more common among women who have been able to surmount sex stereotyping.

Summary

To summarize at this point, career orientation and employment in women are associated with reduced psychological distress, higher self-esteem, and greater instrumentality and coping capacities. The connection of such characteristics to the ability to achieve self-realization and adjustment seems inescapable. That is, people who value themselves, who are capable of instrumental, coping behavior, and who are relatively free from symptoms of depression, anxiety, and fear, are more likely to be able both to recognize and to fulfill their individual potentialities. It is, in essence, a circular phenomenon—people who are able to achieve and fulfill themselves in the outside world as well as the home world feel better about themselves and grow in instrumentality and coping skills. These skills, in turn, facilitate the confidence and willingness to take risks so necessary to further growth and engagement in new areas of endeavor (Yalom, 1985) and thus the continued development of individual potential. This, in turn, should ensure continued movement toward the goal of self-realization.

It should be noted that correlational relationships between career orientation and involvement on the one hand and self-esteem, instrumentality, and adjustment on the other hand do not indicate direction of causality. Although it is most probably true that women with greater self-esteem are better equipped to pursue their goals and to fulfill their capabilities in spite of societal barriers or lack of support, it is also likely that successful career pursuits lead to a maintenance of or an increase in self-esteem. Thus, although the precise causes of the relationship are unknown, the link between career orientation and self-concept is clear.

TOWARD SELF-REALIZATION IN MODERN WOMEN

The initial premise of this chapter postulated the desirability of multiple role involvement, and in particular paid employment, for women as well as for men. This premise is strongly supported by the research reviewed to this point concerning the underutilization of female intelligence and talents in career pursuits and the detrimental effects of this on female adjustment and self-esteem. Thus, it is suggested that for most women involvement in career pursuits is a necessary part of self-realization. The chance to develop and utilize one's unique talents and abilities in the outside world should be available to women as well as to men.

In addition to its desirability for the above mentioned reasons, the fact is that the vast majority of women in modern society do work outside the home for at least part of their adult lives (Betz and Fitzgerald, 1987; Gilbert and Rachlin, 1987), and over 90% of young women today wish to combine career and family pursuits in their adult lives (Rand and Miller, 1972). Thus, it seems that the key to self-realization as well as realization of family values is the chance to combine career and family pursuits. As pointed out by Richardson and Johnson (1984), the interaction of occupational and family roles is one of the most crucial issues concerning women's development—it is an interaction for which there are as yet no explanatory theories or models and about which considerably more knowledge is needed. What can be said at this time, however, is that multiple role involvement has advantages as well as the disadvantages of role conflict and role overload.

Advantages of multiple roles

Often the first reaction to the idea of multiple role involvement in the lives of women has to do with the time-consuming and potentially stressful nature of this involvement. Although time is an issue that must be dealt with (see below), involvement in multiple roles appears to have advantages for both physical and psychological well-being (Baruch and Barnett, 1980; Maracek, Kravetz, and Finn, 1980).

It should be noted first that men have never had to choose between career and family (Gilbert and Rachlin, 1987). One of the most striking findings in the research literature was the strong relationship, at least in past years, between career orientation and marital status in adult women. Research showed career orientation and achievement to be associated with being single versus being married (see Betz and Fitzgerald, 1987; Houseknecht and Spanier, 1980), with deferring marriage (Card et al., 1980), and with having and/or wanting few or no children (Card et al, 1980; Tinsley and Faunce, 1980). Among men, however, marital status has been either unrelated or positively related to achievement—in essence, the more outwardly successful the man, the more likely he is to be married and to have children, while the more outwardly successful the woman, the *less* likely she is to be married and to have children. The vast majority of professional men are married and have children, but the majority of professional women have been single and childless. The discrepancy increases in high-prestige fields traditionally dominated by men, for example, the sciences, law, medicine, and engineering. Since there is strong evidence that these high-level career women come from enriched family backgrounds and had equivalent opportunities for dates and marriage while in college (Almquist, 1974; Sedney and Turner, 1975; Tangri, 1972), one wonders if the pursuit of high-level careers has come with costs for women that were not asked of their male counterparts. Men were able to "have it all," while women are still often forced to choose between home and career.

It seems clear that women should *not* have to choose between career and family. Gove and Tudor (1973), after reviewing extensive research supporting the advantages of men compared to women in mental health, concluded that one of the major reasons for the male advantage was men's involvement in the arenas of both work and family. Similarly, it is now increasingly clear that multiple roles are health-enhancing for women as well. According to a report of data from the U.S. National Center for Health Statistics (cf. Rodgers, 1985), outside work is the strongest predictor of good health for women of all ages, followed by marriage, with children ranking a distant third.

Other research has shown that the benefits to the female spouse in a dual-career couple include the opportunity to develop professionally and to grow and achieve independently from husband and children (to establish a direct rather than a derived sense of identity), economic independence, intellectual companionship and growth, and higher self-esteem (Blumstein and Schwartz, 1983; Gilbert, 1985; Hardesty and Betz, 1980; Sekaran, 1982). In addition, involvement in multiple roles decreases one's vulnerability to loss of one of the roles. The "empty nest" syndrome is a problem primarily for women who have centered their lives on the role of mother. Women who have careers or other significant outside activities where achievement and mastery needs can be met are less vulnerable to the loss of the mother role or of the homemaker role should divorce or the death of a husband occur.

Disadvantages of multiple roles

The most obvious disadvantage of multiple roles is the massive amount of time necessary to fulfill them. The roles of mother and homemaker are certainly time-consuming, and the woman who wishes as well to pursue a career faces the demands of not one but two full-time jobs.

In dealing with this problem it should be said that the fairest solution to the problem of role overload would involve men and women sharing equally in the tasks of home and children, so that each also had an equivalent chance to build his/her career. Research suggests that even though women are now actively pursuing careers, they continue to be responsible for most household and childrearing duties (Gilbert, 1985; St. John Parsons, 1978; Yogev, 1981). In fact, a wife's employment status has little influence on the husband's involvement in family work (Condran and Bode, 1982; Pleck, 1979). The husbands of working women do little more than do the husbands of homemakers, so the assumption remains that "She's free to go to work as long as she can keep up with her responsibilities at home." Thus, women are forced to expend great amounts of time and energy in exchange for the opportunity to pursue their careers.

Until the tasks of the home are shared more equally, the reality that they are not must be dealt with if individual women are to be able to pursue careers that allow opportunities for self-realization. The literature generally mentions approaches to the problem of multiple role overload (e.g. see Gilbert and Holahan, 1982; Gilbert and Rachlin, 1987; Hall, 1972). These approaches are briefly described below.

In structural role redefinition, or what Gilbert (1985) called "role-sharing," the husband as well as the wife is considered responsible for the home and family. This involves sharing of what is known as the executive function (Bem and Bem, 1976) as well as the labor involved. In other words, the husband shares equally in the planning and day-to-day organizing that is required to run a home and raise children.

Personal role redefinition may include cases where the woman decides to reduce her standards of household cleanliness and to reduce her expectations that she can be a perfect mother. On the other hand, increased role behavior (Gilbert and Rachlin, 1987) or greater efficiency (Hall, 1972) involves using better time management and more efficient task-design strategies in order to meet all of the demands of all of the roles. The "superwoman" uses this type of coping strategy (Gilbert and Rachlin, 1987).

Hiring domestic help and locating high-quality childcare can reduce the burden on the woman. Although there is a shortage of high-quality childcare in all Western democracies, comprehensive and generally high-quality systems have been set up in countries such as Israel and France.

For the woman, getting more help from her spouse, children, and/or paid assistants is generally the solution most compatible with her long-term health. Reducing her standards or increasing her efficiency leaves the burden of the home and family responsibilities on her, unfairly restricting her own opportunities for career achievement and self-realization.

SUMMARY AND IMPLICATIONS FOR INTERVENTION

As discussed in the first section of this chapter, there seems to be ample reason to contend that most women, like most men, should be encouraged to pursue rewarding careers. Men have never had to "choose between home and family," and the possibility of combining important life roles is just as vital to the self-realization of women as it is to men. And in their pursuit of careers, women's choices made should represent better matching of their individual characteristics to the level and nature of the chosen field. The waste of female talent and ability when women seriously underutilize their abilities in career choices is a significant personal and societal problem and needs to be counteracted.

Several recommendations for educational and counseling interventions helpful in facilitating women's self-realization can be made (see Betz and Fitzgerald, 1987; Fitzgerald, 1986). Particularly important guidelines for career counseling include the following:

1. Counselors should be knowledgeable in the area of women's career development, including knowledge of research on factors influencing that development and of counselor and test biases that perpetuate stereotyped roles and limited options for women.
2. Counselors should actively encourage the development of a range of interests and competencies, so that choices will truly be "free."
3. Counselors should counteract socialized stereotypes and beliefs that serve to restrict women's range of options, for example, "I can't have both a career and a family," "I can't do math," and "Highly achieving women lose their femininity."

4. Counselors should use materials that help to expand rather than restrict women's range of options, for example, nonsexist interest inventories, vocational card sorts.
5. Counselors should encourage women to obtain quality education and/or training and to gain needed skills in job-hunting, resumé-writing, interviewing, assertion, and information-seeking.
6. Counselors and educators should support women by helping them locate support systems, role models, and mentors.

In addition to these guidelines, Richardson and Johnson (1984) noted that one of the major areas of intervention necessary for the facilitation of women's career development and, thus, opportunities for self-realization is that concerning the integration of occupational and family roles. Intervention strategies are needed which are built upon an appreciation of the difficulties of role integration and which teach strategies for successfully doing so. And although there are as yet no theories or models to guide us, there are some recently developed instruments that counselors and researchers may find useful. These include Tittle's (1981) inventory of values on marriage, family, and occupational roles; Spence and Helmrich's (1978) Work and Family Orientation Questionnaire; Farmer's (1981) measure of Career Motivation and Achievement Planning; and Nevill and Super's (1981) Salience Inventory. A recent special volume on dual-career families (Gilbert, 1987) contains several important articles regarding the counseling of dual-career couples (e.g. Hansen, 1987; O'Neil, Fishman, and Kinsella-Shaw, 1987).

In summary, societal changes leading toward greater labor force participation and career achievement among women should have positive effects on women's self-realization and psychological adjustment. It is hoped that the ideas presented in this chapter will contribute to both understanding of the issues facing women in the task of self-realization and to the effective use of intervention strategies which may assist women in their realization of their abilities and talents and their integration of career achievement and family roles.

REFERENCES

Abrahams, B., Feldman, S. S., and Nash, S. C. 1978. Sex role, self concept, and sex role attitudes. *Developmental Psychology*, 14: 399–400.

Almquist, E. M. 1974. Sex stereotypes in occupational choice: The case for college women. *Journal of Vocational Behavior*, 5: 13–21.

Anastasi, A. 1965. *Individual Differences*. New York: John Wiley.

Astin, H. S. 1984. The meaning of work in women's lives. *The Counseling Psychologist*, 12: 117–126.

Bachtold, L. M. 1976. Personality characteristics of women of distinction. *Psychology of Women Quarterly*, 1: 70–78.

Bachtold, L. M., and Werner, E. E. 1970. Personality profiles of gifted women: Psychologists. *American Psychologist*, 25: 234–243.

Bakan, D. 1966. *The Duality of Human Existence: An Essay on Psychology and Religion*. Chicago: Rand McNally.

Barron, F., and Welsh, G. S. 1952. Artistic perception as a possible factor in personality style: Its measurement by a figure preference test. *Journal of Psychology*, 33: 199–203.

Bart, P. 1971. Depression in middle aged women. In V. Gornich and B. K. Moran (Eds.), *Women in Sexist Society*. New York: New American Library, pp. 163–186.

Baruch, G. K. 1976. Girls who perceive themselves as competent: Some antecedents and correlates. *Psychology of Women Quarterly*, 1: 38–49.

Baruch, G. K., and Barnett, R. C. 1980. On the well-being of adult women. In L. A. Bond and J. C. Rosen (Eds.), *Competence and Coping During Adulthood*. Hanover, N.H.: University Press of New England, pp. 240–257.

Bem, S. J. 1974. The measurement of psychological androgyny. *Journal of Consulting and Clinical Psychology*, 42: 155–162.

Bem, S. J. 1977. On the utility of alternate procedures for assessing psychological androgyny. *Journal of Consulting and Clinical Psychology*, 45: 196–205.

Bem, S. L., and Bem, D. J. 1976. Case study of a non-conscious ideology: Training the woman to know her place. In S. Cox (Ed.), *Female Psychology*. Chicago: Science Research Associates, pp. 180–191.

Berk, R. A., and Berk, S. F. 1979. *Labor and Leisure at Home*. Beverly Hills, Calif.: Sage.

Bernard, J. 1971. The paradox of the happy marriage. In V. Gornick and B. K. Moran (Eds.), *Woman in Sexist Society*. New York: New American Library, pp. 145–162.

Betz, N. E., and Fitzgerald, F. L. 1987. *The Career Psychology of Women*. New York: Academic Press.

Betz, N. E., Fitzgerald, L. F., and Hill, R. E. 1989. Trait-factor theories: Foundations of career theory. In D. T. Hall, M. Arthur, and B. S. Lawrence (Eds.), *Handbook of Career Theory*. Cambridge: Oxford University Press.

Blumstein, P., and Schwartz, P. 1983. *American Couples: Money, Work, and Sex*. New York: William Morrow.

Card, J. J., Steel, L., and Abeles, R. P. 1980. Sex differences in the realization of individual potential for achievement. *Journal of Vocational Behavior*, 17: 1–21.

Carnegie Commission on Higher Education. 1973. *Opportunities for Women in Higher Education*. New York: McGraw-Hill.

Castle, C. S. 1913. A statistical study of eminent women. *Archives of Psychology*, 27: 20–34.

Cattell, R. B., Eber, H. W., and Tatsuoka, M. M. 1970. *Manual for Forms A and B: Sixteen Personality Factor Questionnaire*. Champaign, Ill.: Institute for Personality Testing.

Condran, J. G., and Bode, J. G. 1982. Rashomon, working wives, and family division of labor: Middletown, 1980. *Journal of Marriage and the Family*, 44: 421–426.

Cook, E. P. 1985. *Psychological Androgyny*. New York: Pergamon.

Coopersmith, S. 1967. *The antecedents of Self-Esteem*. San Francisco: Freeman.

Crites, J. O. 1969. *Vocational Psychology.* New York: McGraw-Hill.

Crites, J. O. 1978. *Career Maturity Inventory: Theory and Research Handbook.* Monterey, Calif.: CTB/McGraw-Hill.

Eiduson, B.T. 1958. Artist and nonartist: A comparative study. *Journal of Personality,* 26: 13–28.

Erikson, E. 1950. *Childhood and Society.* New York: Norton.

Falk, W. W., and Cosby, A. G. 1978. Women's marital-familial statuses and work histories: Some conceptual considerations. *Journal of Vocational Behavior,* 13: 126–140.

Farmer, H. S. 1976. What inhibits achievement and career motivation in women? *The Counseling Psychologist,* 6: 12–14.

Farmer, H. S. 1981. *The Development of a Measure of Career Motivation and Achievement Planning for Both Sexes.* Paper presented at the annual meeting of the American Psychological Association, Los Angeles.

Ferree, M. M. 1976. The confused American housewife. *Psychology Today,* 10: 76–80.

Fiske, M., and Weiss, L. 1977. Intimacy and crises in adulthood. In N. K. Schlossberg and A. D. Entine (Eds.), *Counseling Adults.* Monterey, Calif.: Brooks/Cole, pp. 19–33.

Fitzgerald, L. F. 1986. Career counseling women. In Z. Leibowitz and D. Lee (Eds.), *Adult Career Development.* Washington, D.C.: National Vocational Guidance Association.

Fitzgerald, L. F., and Betz, N. E. 1983. Issues in the vocational psychology of women. In W. B. Walsh and S. H. Osipow (Eds.), *Handbook of Vocational Psychology,* Vol. I. Hillsdale, N.J.: Lawrence Erlbaum.

Fitzgerald, L. F., and Crites, J. O. 1980. Toward a career psychology of women. *Journal of Counseling Psychology,* 27: 44–62.

Flanagan, J. C. 1971. *Project TALENT: Five Years After High School and Appendix II Final Report.* Pittsburgh: University of Pittsburgh, American Institutes for Research.

Gaddy, C. D., Glass, C. R., and Arnkoff, D. B. 1983. Career development of women in dual career families: The influence of sex role identity. *Journal of Counseling Psychology,* 30: 388–394.

Ghiselli, E. E. 1971. *Explorations in Managerial Talent.* Pacific Palisades, Calif.: Goodyear Publishing.

Gilbert, L. A. 1981. Toward mental health: The benefits of psychological androgyny. *Professional Psychology,* 12: 29–38.

Gilbert, L. A. 1985. *Men in Dual Career Families: Current Realities and Future Prospects.* Hillsdale, N.J.: Lawrence Erlbaum.

Gilbert, L. A., and Holahan, C. K. 1982. Conflicts between student/professional, parental, and self-developmental roles: A comparison of high and low effective copers. *Human Relations,* 35: 635–648.

Gilbert, L. A., and Rachlin, V. 1987. Mental health and psychological functioning of dual career families. *The Counseling Psychologist,* 15: 7–49.

Gottfredson, L. S. 1981. Circumscription and compromise: A developmental theory of occupational aspirations. *Journal of Counseling Psychology,* 28: 545–579.

Gough, H. G. 1957. *Manual for the California Psychological Inventory.* Palo Alto, Calif.: Consulting Psychologists Press.

Gove, W. R., and Tudor, J. F. 1973. Adult sex roles and mental illness. *American Journal of Sociology*, 78: 812–835.

Greenglass, E. R., and Devins, R. 1982. Factors related to marriage and career plans in unmarried women. *Sex Roles*, 8: 57–72.

Greenhaus, J. H., and Simon, W. E. 1976. Self-esteem, career salience, and the choice of an ideal occupation. *Journal of Vocational Behavior*, 8: 51–58.

Hall, D. T. 1972. A model of coping with role conflict: The role behavior of college educated women. *Administrative Science Quarterly*, 17: 471–489.

Hansen, C. S. 1987. Career socialization, social change, prevention: Critical issues for dual career counseling. *Counseling Psychologist*, 15: 122–130.

Hardesty, S. A., and Betz, N. E. 1981. The relationships of career salience, attitudes toward women, and demographic and family characteristics to marital adjustment in dual career couples. *Journal of Vocational Behavior*, 17: 242–248.

Hoffman, L. 1977. Changes in family roles, socialization, and sex differences. *American Psychologist*, 32: 644–657.

Houseknecht, S. K., and Spanier, G. S. 1980. Marital disruption and higher education among women in the United States. *The Sociological Quarterly*, 21: 375–389.

Hyde, J. S. (1981). How large are cognitive gender differences? *American Psychologist*, 36: 892–901.

Hyde, J. S. (1985). *Half the Human Experience: The Psychology of Women*, 3rd ed. Lexington, Mass.: D. C. Heath.

Ilfeld, F., Jr. 1977. *Sex Differences in Psychiatric Symptomatology*. Paper presented at the meeting of the American Psychological Association, San Francisco.

Lemkau, J. P. 1979. Personality and background characteristics of women in male-dominated occupations: A review. *Psychology of Women Quarterly*, 4: 221–240.

Lemkau, J. P. (1983). Women in male-dominated professions: Distinguishing personality and background characteristics. *Psychology of Women Quarterly*, 8: 144–165.

Lowenthal, M. F., Thurnher, M., and Chiriboga, D. 1975. *Four Stages of Life*. San Francisco: Jossey Bass.

Maccoby, E. E., and Jacklin, C. N. 1974. *The Psychology of Sex Differences*. Stanford, Calif.: Stanford University Press.

MacKinnon, D. W. 1962. The nature and nurture of creative talent. *American Psychologist*, 17: 484–495.

Maracek, J., Kravetz, D., and Finn, S. 1980. *Labor Force Participation and Women's Psychological Well-being*. Paper presented at the meeting of the Eastern Psychological Association, Hartford, Connecticut.

Maslow, A. H. 1954. *Motivation and Personality*. New York: Harper.

Matthews, E., and Tiedeman, D. V. 1964. Attitudes toward career and marriage and the development of lifestyle in young women. *Journal of Counseling Psychology*, 11: 374–383.

Nevill, D. D., and Super, D. E. 1986. *The Salience Inventory Manual (Research Edition)*. Palo Alto, Calif.: Consulting Psychologists Press.

O'Neil, J. M., Fishman, D. M., and Kinsella-Shaw, M. 1987. Dual-career couples, career transitions, and normative dilemmas. *The Counseling Psychologist*, 15: 50–96.

Orlovsky, J. L., and Stake, J. E. 1981. Psychological masculinity and femininity: Relationship to striving and self-concept in the achievement and interpersonal domains. *Psychology of Women Quarterly*, 6: 218–233.

Osipow, S. H. 1983. *Theories of Career Development*, 3rd ed. New York: Prentice Hall.

Parsons, F. 1909. *Choosing a Vocation*. Boston: Houghton Mifflin.

Perun, P. J., and Bielby, D. 1981. Toward a model of female occupational behavior: A human developmental approach. *Psychology of Women Quarterly*, 6: 234–252.

Pleck, J. H. 1979. Men's family work: Three perspectives and some new data. *Family Coordinator*, 28: 481–488.

Radloff, L. 1975. Sex differences in depression: The effects of occupation and marital status. *Sex Roles*, 1: 249–265.

Rand, L. M., and Miller, A. L. 1972. A developmental cross-sectioning of women's careers and marriage attitudes and life plans. *Journal of Vocational Behavior*, 2: 317–331.

Richardson, M. S., and Johnson, M. 1984. Counseling women. In S. Brown and R. Lent (Eds.), *Handbook of Counseling Psychology*. New York: Wiley, pp. 832–877.

Ridgeway, C. L., and Jacobsen, C. K. 1979. The development of female role ideology: Impact of personal confidence during adolescence. *Youth and Society*, 10: 297–315.

Rodgers, J. E. 1985. The best health kick of all. *Ms.*, May, pp. 57–60.

Roe, A. 1951a. A psychological study of eminent biologists. *Psychological Monographs*, 65(14): 1–58.

Roe, A. 1951b. A psychological study of physical scientists. *Genetic Psychology Monographs*, 43: 121–235.

Roe, A. 1953. A psychological study of eminent psychologists and anthropologists and a comparison with eminent biological and physical scientists. *Psychological Monographs*, 67(2): 1–55.

Rogers, C. 1951. *Client Centered Therapy*. Boston: Houghton Mifflin.

Rosenberg, M. 1965. *Society and the Adolescent Self-Image*. Princeton, N.J.: Princeton University Press.

Rosenberg, M. 1979. *Conceiving the Self*. New York: Basic Books.

Sears, P. S., and Barbie, A. H. 1977. Career and life satisfaction among Terman's gifted women. In J. C. Stanley, W. George, and C. Solano (Eds.), *The Gifted and Creative: Fifty Year Perspective*. Baltimore, Md.: Johns Hopkins University Press.

Seashore, C. E. 1939. *Psychology of Music*. New York: McGraw-Hill.

Sedney, M. A., and Turner, B. F. 1975. A test of causal sequences in two models of the development of career orientation in women. *Journal of Vocational Behavior*, 6: 281–291.

Sekaran, U. 1982. An investigation of the career salience of men and women in dual career families. *Journal of Vocational Behavior*, 20: 111–119.

Spence, J. T., and Helmreich, R. L. 1978. The Work and Family Orientation Questionnaire. *Journal Supplements Abstract Service (JSAS)*.

Spence, J. T., and Helmreich, R. L. 1980. Masculine instrumentality and feminine expressiveness: Their relationships with sex role attitudes and behaviors. *Psychology of Women Quarterly*, 5: 147–153.

Spence, J. T., Helmreich, R. L., and Stapp. J. 1975. Ratings of self and peers on sex role attributes and their relation to self-esteem and conceptions of masculinity and femininity. *Journal of Personality and Social Psychology*, 32: 29–39.

Stericker, A. B., and Johnson, J. E. 1977. Sex role identification and self-esteem in college students. Do men and women differ? *Sex Roles*, 3: 19–26.

St. John Parsons, D. 1978. Continuous dual-career families: A case study. *Psychology of Women Quarterly*, 3: 30–42.

Super, D. E. 1957. *The Psychology of Careers*. New York: Harper.

Super, D. E. 1963. Self-concepts in vocational development. In D. E. Super, R. Starishevshy, N. Martin, and J. P. Jordaan (Eds.), *Career Development: Self Concept Theory*. New York: CEEB Research Monograph, No. 4.

Super, D. E. 1980. A life-span, life-space approach to career development. *Journal of Vocational Behavior,* 16: 282–298.

Tangri, S. 1972. Determinants of occupational role innovation among college women. *Journal of Social Issues*, 28: 177–199.

Terman, L. M., and Oden, M. H. 1959. *Genetic Studies of Genius. V: The Gifted Group at Midlife*. Stanford, Calif.: Stanford University Press.

Tinsley, D. J., and Faunce, P. S. 1980. Enabling, facilitating, and precipitating factors associated with women's career orientation. *Journal of Vocational Behavior*, 17: 183–194.

Tittle, C. K. 1981. *Sex Differences in Occupational Values*. Paper presented at the annual meeting of the American Psychological Association, Los Angeles.

Tyler, L. E. 1965. *The Psychology of Human Differences*. New York: Appleton-Century-Crofts.

Tyler, L. E. 1978. *Individuality*. San Francisco: Jossey Bass.

Wells, L. E., and Marwell, G. 1976. *Self-Esteem: Its Conceptualization and Measurement*. Beverly Hills, Calif.: Sage.

Wolfe, L. K., and Betz, N. E. 1981. Traditionality of choice and sex role identification as moderators of the congruence of occupational choice in college women. *Journal of Vocational Behavior*, 18: 43–55.

"Women Cut Aims, Study of Honors Students Show." 1987. Chicago: Associated Press, May 15.

Wong, P. T. P., Kettlewell, G., and Sproule, C. F. 1985. On the importance of being masculine: Sex role, attribution, and women's career achievement. *Sex Roles*, 12: 757–768.

Wylie, R. C. 1979. *The Self-Concept: Theory and Research on Selected Topics*. Lincoln: University of Nebraska Press.

Yalom, I. 1985. *Existential Psychotherapy*. New York: Basic Books.

Yogev, S. 1981. Do professional women have egalitarian marital relationships? *Journal of Marriage and the Family*, 43: 865–871.

9

The Vocational Project and the Planning of Training in the Framework of a Life Project

Pierre L. G. Goguelin

The vocational project constitutes a new experience linked to mental evolution in industrially advanced countries. We define the concept, to see how it is possible to implement it positively and inscribe it in the development of society.

There is already a clear separation between project and foreseeing, the latter implying knowledge of the future with a certain degree of certitude. Before clarifying the notion of a project, we have to separate it from two other notions: that of hope and that of choice. In fact, further on, we will see that psychologists have often created confusion on this subject by seeking to establish inventories of attitudes or questionnaires of professional interests.

A hope is a desire for oneself, expressed or not, to obtain something or to see an event occur. It is generally a one-off thing or event, to be realized in one go. In the semantic field, we find as synonyms: aspiration (action of carrying desires toward an ideal),[1] longing (desire to have), and wish (hope that something will come about, often addressed to a deity). Thus the word "hope" summons up the imaginary. To ask someone what he hopes to do—vocationally—later, is to ask him to imagine an ideal without taking into account the means of achievement. In French folklore, when on a beautiful summer night you see a shooting star, you must formulate a hope, a wish, "which will be granted"—I hoped to win in the lottery, but even so, I didn't win.

A choice is the operation by which we show a preference for one thing ("it corresponds to our tastes"), discarding the others. This implies that the things from which we choose are well defined, well known, real: "what would you choose to be: a fireman or a policeman?" Choice takes place in the here and now; but choice is not decision, which is something marking the end of deliberation, in a voluntary act of doing or not doing. Choice exists in a reversible universe whereas decision transfers us to an irreversible universe.

What therefore is a project?[2] It is the image of a future situation, of a state you consider attainable.[3] This implies that the situation, the state, may be as of now sufficiently well defined to provide a direction for action and that this future may also be sufficiently realistic and realizable. However, a project is not a plan (or a strategy), which, on the contrary, may be formulated in order to realize the project.

THE VOCATIONAL PROJECT AND SELF-REALIZATION

The vocational project is thus the mental representation of a future vocational situation that we think can be attained. Naturally "future" includes the short range as well as the medium or long range.

In the short range we can imagine someone who loses his job because his work is no longer economically viable (e.g. a steel worker) and who tries to define a possible alternative. What is essential for him is to extricate himself from a difficult situation, any long-range project seeming to him to be unrealistic.

In the medium range, let us consider someone who, when starting a company, tries to define what he wants to achieve within that company. This may be a vocational project lasting 5, 10, or 15 years. But this project can benefit from being integrated into a long-range project.

In the long range, the project is one lasting a lifetime—that is, it is one for which we are capable of defining a final aim to be attained as we have a sufficiently complete view of the stages required for its accomplishment. The concrete realization may thus be:

- either a succession of medium-range projects leading to the long-range realization, especially if the fact of reaching the final aim implies different knowledge and experience that can only be acquired by changing the job, specialty, or company several times;
- or a continuous unfolding of the same project, which implies a development in the same sphere of knowledge or experience and/or a progression in the same company.

Be it a short-, medium-, or long-range vocational project, it is clear that it will require new attainments, and these attainments must be there at the required moment in order to realize the project or the stage of the project. Thus necessarily at the beginning the vocational project doubles as a training project which must quickly transform itself, at least in the short or medium range, into a genuine training plan.

One question then arises: is life organized entirely around one single vocational project? It is obvious that there is no one answer: the situation is not the same for the person without family responsibilities as for those who have started a family for which they are responsible. And, for those who have a family, everything will depend on the burden of this family life (of the family project, if we might say that) in relation to other projects.

All of us, even if unconsciously, have a global project for life, which we would hardly be able to explain, and which is often in conflict with our inner selves (and between corresponding projects in different spheres), but in terms of which we make our decisions. This takes us straight back to success and self-realization.

As far as success is concerned, the vocational project can lead to vocational success: the training project and the training plan can lead to "academic" success in its widest sense (success at any age in the acquisition of new knowledge): the project for life can lead to family, economic or social success, and so forth. The observer will say of the man who accumulates these successes: he has *succeeded*. But we have already seen that he may have *succeeded* and yet consider himself to have wasted his life, not to have realized himself.

As far as self-realization is concerned, what is essential for the individual is not a third-party judgment on the value of his life, but the judgment of values (including emotional values) that s/he him/herself passes on his/her own past. Without embarking on a philosophical discussion, the fact of having succeeded can bring satisfaction, but only the realization of oneself can bring "happiness," the feeling of fulfillment.

THE TRADITIONAL HELP IN A VOCATIONAL PROJECT

We cannot separate the vocational project from the training project, which is itself linked to the organization of teaching and education in society. These three aspects, which were linked at the beginning, then separated from one another during the evolution of society.

If we go back to the last century, a person's working life started early, from the age of 13 in the majority of cases and often even earlier. The family decided for the child. The social class, the family's financial resources, were the determining factors, because the family had no means of supporting the cost of a child's education.[4] The work of the eldest, when large families were still a common feature, was to bring up the youngest. The paternal influence was great, the work market was limited to the town or the village, the possiblities of choice for the adolescent were limited. Once he had started work, days of 10 hours or more, weeks of 60 hours, did not leave him much time for thinking or for leisure. Anyway, without any guidance on what he might do, the man of that period was practically doomed to pursue the way laid down for him. The only vocational project he could envisage was to be successful in his work. This was the heart of the quantitative period.

From 1882, a new character appeared in French society: the primary school teacher. Faced with the family which was ill-informed and in which economic preoccupations were a determining factor, the primary school teacher was able to discover the gifted pupils who were capable of pursuing their studies. Little by little a system of help, of grants, was established, making it possible to relieve the family of the financial burden the continuation of studies placed on it. A dialogue was established between the teacher, who spoke on behalf of the child, and the family. But, with certain exceptions, this young person had not yet enough information to formulate a vocational project that would be his own: the part played by the teacher (the pedagogue) in the decision to be taken was of prime importance.

From 1905 to 1914, and again after the First World War, the context changed. In relation to the generation of the 1880s, we have reached the second generation; in 1919 the law estabished working hours at 8 hours a day, and the Astier Law established a framework for technical teaching; the standard of living rose, grants were more numerous. But psychologists also came on the scene. In 1906 Alfred Binet published his metric scale of intelligence (IQ), taken over by Terman in 1916. After J. MacKeen Cattell's "mental tests,"[5] a new idea saw the light of day[6] and was applied in 1919: the idea that it was possible "to guide" the young toward the jobs that best suited them and in which they had the greatest chance of success. In France, vocational guidance started in private centers as early as 1920, becoming compulsory (1938) for all young people under 17 who wished to enter an industrial or commercial occupation.

This period was therefore marked by the appearance of a fourth character: apart from the adolescent, his/her family, and the teacher, there was now the vocational counselor. The ideas of that time were that, in order to prevent failure, it was necessary to advise the adolescents—and their parents—in which work they had the best chances of success, and in which they had the greatest probabilities of failure. The master word is "aptitude": "have they the aptitudes necessary for . . .?" Examinations using psychometric tests would be developed to measure the so-called aptitudes, and studies would be launched on the major occupations in order to detect, for each of them, the level in each of the required aptitudes; the implicit idea was that, if one had aptitudes, then one must succeed. Guy Sinoir (1943), one of the French pioneers, described the typical professional guidance file in the chapter "Determination of Aptitudes":

1.   The physical and physiological aptitudes: physiological record and medical record.

2. Psychological aptitudes: psychological record: motor function, mental level, discussion with the child;[7]
3. Psychosocial aptitudes: academic record and family record (discussion with the parents).

In other words, the primary school teacher fades away, and the two main decision-makers become the parents and the professional counselor; the children are "officially" consulted very little, and they receive no help in their search for a vocational project, only being informed of their aptitudes.

From the 1930s, American psychologists became interested in motivation. G. F. Kuder, for example, had elaborated an inventory test of individual preferences regarding ten main spheres of professional activity; G. W. Allport and Ph. E. Vernon had perfected a scale for the study of values. These studies were followed by many others which required the subjects either to express their hopes or to make choices. The analysis of the hopes and choices provides an indication of preferences that can be used as a basis for subjects' life projects and vocational projects, the basis of their self-realization. In Europe, these tests began to be used only in the 1960s; this more or less corresponds to the period when we started to talk about the quality of life. In reality the phenomenon is very complex: activities and social conditions had evolved considerably; the family standard of living rose again when secondary education became free (from 1929 in France), as also in most cases did higher education[8] with many grants;[9] school was made compulsory until the age of 16 (1959), with the result that adolescents were much more mature when they came to elaborate their vocational projects: psychologists and parents had become aware that an adolescent could have good academic results, be guided toward an occupation for which s/he had the required ability, but then fail—and vice versa.[10] Finally, in-service training for adults has made such progress[11] that ample possibilities were offered to anyone who had a vocational project and was ready to realize it him/herself.[12] The conditions were therefore met, allowing people to think of their development.

During this period much research was carried out aimed at establishing or adapting tests for interests, attitudes, tastes, preferences, and so on. This research strengthened the arsenal of psychometric tests, and it was thus possible to have a dialogue with the subject about his/her overall results. Progress was perceptible as the subject was put in a situation of getting to know him/herself better and thus his/her long-term choices were made clearer. Let us note that, fortunately, a certain correlation exists between aptitude and taste (or preference) at least within a choice made by the subject.

In 1963, the author had the opportunity to distribute about 100 eighteen-year-olds into five different types of vocational training corresponding to five occupations. The experiment was exceptional, as this guidance took place after the teenagers had each worked on a trial basis in each of the specialties for a whole month. We had at our disposal the results during these five "occupational try-outs" of their replies to a simple question: "If you had the possibility to choose, which would be your first choice and which your second choice out of the five specialties?" (which would subsequently have the same status and identical remuneration). Also available were the results of a set of aptitude tests sufficient to provide guidance, by aptitude, toward one of the five specialties. The personal choices of each corresponded, with very little deviation, to their academic results (which they ignored) and to the psychotechnical classification carried out without their knowledge: all of them had, therefore, a tendency to go toward the activity that best corresponded to their tastes and aptitudes, where they felt they would succeed best and have the most satisfaction. It would no doubt be dangerous to generalize from a very partial study, but we can say that when people have some information on themselves and the possibilities that are offered and they must make choices, they do not do it by chance and whatever the circumstances, they do it rather well, bearing in mind what they are like, thus showing a certain inner coherence. However, they must have enough elements of information: it is therefore quite right that vocational counselors in France have become "vocational guidance and information counselors."

NEW CONCEPTIONS OF HELP TO THE VOCATIONAL PROJECT: TOWARDS NEO-COUNSELING

Until the 1970s, the help given to a vocational project was mainly focused on the adolescent or the very young adult, as we have just seen. Certainly, a 30- or 40-year-old adult might come to us to "sum up the situation," that is, in reality, to try to build a new starting platform; but this was rare, and the difficulties were most often to be found at the level of the subject's more or less psychopathic personality. For a long time, personality was considered by the vocational counselors, as well as by the selectors, as of secondary importance, that is, the psychologist had to suspect something was important to bring himelf to carry out a more thorough examination. Projective tests, it is true, were long and delicate. We now possess many well-designed inventories of personality.[13]

Now, if a vocational project is one of the elements of the life project leading to self-realization, the life project is inconceivable if there is no deep agreement between it and the personality. "Head hunters" take great care to penetrate the personality of the candidate through multiple interviews during which discussions are more often on the candidate's hobbies than on their technical capacities.

For the last fifteen years, the Western world has been in a period of depression; the oil crisis has made us reconsider an expansion that had been continuous for 30 years; new technologies appear every day either replacing man by machines or so modifying traditional work that a professionally competent person ceases to be such, not always having the capacity to acquire the new competence. We are faced with a considerable problem of adult re-cycling and placing of young people.[14]

Apart from those who already have work and for whom the problem of their vocational project arises normally, about 3,000,000 people in France are traumatized either by the loss of their job, often because it just disappears, or by their incapacity to find a job corresponding to the training they have received. Incidentally, the social effort made to recycle these workers is considerable: it would be particularly stupid not to do it as well as possible. The idea of a "continuous vocational guidance" is developing: we are becoming aware of the fact that people's lives must, through all the changes, from childhood to old age, enjoy continuity (which does not mean uniformity). This continuity, if it is well managed, can take them at least to success—even, hopefully, to their own realization.

In order to encourage the self-realization of people, both in and by way of their work, a body of neo-counselors must be created.[15] These would be independent psychologists offering their services to the public and also, possibly, freelance workers in companies who would be available to any person hoping to take stock of his/her development.

In no way will psychotherapies, even short ones, be carried out by the neo-counselor, and he/she will have to refuse them if they are requested and send the person to a professional psychotherapist. The psychologist–patient relationship will be clearly and solely established in terms of facilitation of the client's problem study, essentially eased by a search for information. The study of the problem and the search for information must be conducted by the client and the psychologist together, the latter trying to make the client progress toward his/her aims within his/her own structure.

The work of the neo-counselor could, then, be described thus: the psychologist will seek the maximum information from the client, from the most global and profound to the field of aptitudes and capacities[16] and then hand back the information to the subject, encouraging him/her at each stage to draw conclusions for him/herself, integrating any new conclusion into the previously drawn ones. The psychologist will make sure that no contradictions or conflicts remain, which must be clarified each time, confronted with the reality, and from which options must be *freely* taken by the subject. In fact, the essential condition on which to base a vocational project in the framework of a life projects is to reach a balance, a consensus or an inner coherence sufficient in the subject to enable him/her to determine his/her aims. And these should be sufficiently permanent aims, for, in order to decide what to do, it is first necessary to know where we want to go. Any other strategy is doomed to failure.

The order of compiling and retrojection of information in the framework of the permanent integration process above would be as follows:

(1) The psychologist facilitates the elucidation by the subject of his/her ideal of life. To do this s/he can make his/her patient "talk and reflect," most often using a nondirective technique, stimulating talk by relying on scenes (photographs, drawings), on very short accounts of the lives of very typical individuals or of well-known people, real ("historical," present-day) or fictional (novels, films, actors, etc.), who might be admired or rejected by the subject, and then by making him/her describe his/her personal ideal and above all what s/he does not want to be—and, if possible, why.

(2) The psychologist "examines" the subject with the help of well-known tests: questionnaires on personality and temperament, personal adaptation to different types of situation including resistance to stress or the subject's creative capacity; then, questionnaires aimed at determining the subject's scales of values and attitudes (including his/her individual architectonics in the sense of G. A. Kelly); finally, questionnaires of interests, preferences, and professional choice. After each test, the subjects must be able to express agreement or disagreement and link the information they have been given to their daily lives: it is in fact fundamental that it is the subjects themselves and they alone who can resolve their problems and not the psychologist. The latter is there only to help them spell out the details of their problems as clearly as possible.

(3) The psychologist will help the subjects to confront their ideals with their real capacities in order to realize them: s/he will therefore draw up the most exhaustive list possible of the aptitudes using psychotechnical tests. Some of these tests will be taken in their psychometric form in order to establish the capacity level of the subject, others will be taken in permanent dialogue with the subject using a more clinical approach. There are thousands of ways of satisfying a personality trait, a temperamental factor, centers of interest: it is better to succeed first—and perhaps realize oneself—as a nurse, than to be bitter all one's life because one hoped to succeed in medicine and in fact became a bank clerk. The knowledge of the neo-counselor can be very useful in suggesting counterpropositions for what will most probably be inaccessible: his/her role is to open subjects' minds to other "things" that they might not otherwise have thought of.

(4) The psychologist will also, together with the subject, sum up the latter's economic possibilities and his/her present social status and possibilities, taking into account any constraints and what it is necessary to do to surpass these "barriers." This last point is very important: it is a matter of judging the will power of the subjects, their tenacity, their reaction when faced with an obstacle, which takes us back to the tests in stage (3).

When these four stages have been covered, while at the same time making sure of their progressive integration, the time will have come to ask the question: what is to be done to satisfy points (1) and (2) while taking into account the constraints in (3) and (4)?

The answer is complex: the reflection must relate to the global life project, integrating the vocational project and the socioeconomic project. Throughout this work toward maturity, which cannot take place in one day, the neo-counselor must beware of subjects' stereotypes, of everything that might be prompted by their own families, by habits and social customs; s/he must clearly reveal them so that the subjects can make decisions in relation to themselves and by themselves alone, and if they make concessions to others, they must do it consciously.[17] If possible, they should prepare a plan, a schedule for realization, and this schedule must be realistic.

THE VOCATIONAL PROJECT AND THE TRAINING PROJECT

If we exclude the case of people who conclude that they are at peace with themselves and the way they are, and they have no desire to change, the subject is generally in a situation different from the one s/he wants to reach and in which s/he sees the possibility of realizing him/herself.

If we take only the vocational project into account, the subject must take responsibility for it, acquiring what s/he lacks in knowledge as well as in know-how about how to appear and how to be. The subject must build a training project that will materialize, in the form of a plan, a schedule for his training. We must once again note the full importance (and not the influence!) of the neo-counsellor, whose knowledge may help the subject in this elaboration.

To train is to produce new contents and a formal structure at the same time, that is, to give birth, create life, animate, which is not connected with the ultimate idea of self-realization; the formal structure promotes the particular and concrete realization of a general abstract fact, a concept, an idea that is not unconnected with success.

To train thus is to provide the means of transferring the ideal of life to the actual life. The training project anticipates the dynamics of "actualization," which consists of statically establishing the training plan. This must favor the success of the vocational project and the overall self-realization at the same time. Now, we have always been struck by the fact that, when we systematically asked the employees of a company "what kind of training would you like, what training program would be useful to you?" we obtained only short-range utilitarian answers, lacking in originality (e.g. further technical training because the person thinks it will look good, or foreign language courses corresponding to the country where s/he spends her/his holidays). We therefore note a kind of incapacity to set one's own problem of development and fulfilment. In reality, the person has not got the feeling of being master of his fate but of submitting to the will of others or to economic and social constraints. The moment of truth will sometimes appear later, as we have already seen, at the time of retirement, but then it will be too late.

The training plan raises three successive questions which the subject must answer:

1.   What programs must I assimilate in order to reach my goal?
2.   How and where can I do it practically: what are the strategies to be put into effect, taking my constraints into account?
3.   At what moment in time must I have acquired these programs?

The establishment of the training plan and its follow-up by the neo-counselor with the subjects's agreement will be the best test of the latter's will to succeed.

TOWARDS A BODY OF NEO-COUNSELORS: GUIDANCE AND IN-SERVICE TRAINING CONSULTANTS

It is very difficult—except in the case of early and true vocational calling—to discover by ourselves, alone, what we want to become, to know how, through what channels, it will be possible to realize ourselves and how to achieve it practically.

It is therefore urgent to set up a body of neo-counselors who could call themselves "guidance and in-service training consultants,"[18] having clearly stated that their essential brief is to help the greatest number of people to reflect, to sum up their situation, to build a future and a development that would lead them at least to success and, if possible to full self-realization.

Naturally these consultants ought to have, in addition to an excellent psychological training (both experimental and clinical), very good information about the labor market and about qualifications—especially those linked to developing new techniques.

To "counsel" a person will no doubt mean to devote three whole days to him in the first year, with half-day "boosters" aimed at regulating the cohesion of the subject's progression. This represents an eight-day investment per person. It is quite a heavy process; is it realistic?

If we consider the minimum academic training (in France), the average child attends school for 12 to 14 years; if s/he continues to higher education, we must add 8 years, i.e. 20 to 22 years. Assuming 30 subjects per "class," the amount of time that the average subject requires from an adult (primary- and secondary-school teachers) for him/herself in 14/30 years is about 6 months. The gifted subject requires 20/30 years, or 9 months, from an adult (primary- and secondary-school teachers, then university lecturers).

If we now consider the 35 to 40 years of active life, if we take into account the wasted time, the hindrances of all kinds that are the consequence of people being indifferent and sometimes unhappy in their work, those years are wasted for the person, the company, and society—and we have seen that more than one person out of two is in this category.

Faced with this enormous human waste, would it be so stupid to invest eight days per person, that is to say, perhaps 3 percent more than what is at present allocated?

A pilot experiment is called for![19]

NOTES

1. See further on, the link with the ideal ego.

2. From the Latin, *projectus* meaning thrown forwards.

3. The philosophical definition of project is wider and covers "all the reasons why man tends to modify the world or himself in a given way."

4. The French Revolution (1971–1793) established three teaching levels: primary, secondary, and higher. In 1808, secondary and higher education came under the control of the state, but primary remained under the control of the church. Primary schooling was not compulsory, and children from poor families rarely went to school. In 1881 primary education became compulsory, nondenominational, and free to everyone.

5. In the magazine *Mind*, 1890.

6. An idea defended by Sharp in 1899: individuals can be differentiated by their higher aptitudes.

7. In Guy Sinoir's text, these interviews seem reduced to the minimum, and on the whole they took place when the tests were taken.

8. French students currently pay about $70 (U.S.) registration fee to the university per year, whatever the number of courses followed. There are no restrictions on entry.

9. 150,000 grants for 1,000,000 students.

10. See interview in *Le Figaro* with the mother of Mathias Rust, the young man who landed his Cessna in Red Square, Moscow, on 28 May 1987: "The only thing in his head was flying. We really tried to make him join a bank when he left school, but it didn't work out that way. Flying was what interested him."

11. The 1971 law on vocational training: in 1985, 4,000,000 salaried staff (i.e. 1 in 6) benefitted from free training, during working hours, for 120 hours on average.

12. We have not mentioned here, although it is very interesting, the universities (34) for retired people, open since 1973 to all elderly people, without any conditions of entry. It would seem that many of these elderly people went there precisely to do what they would have liked to have done during their occupational lives: they went to realize themselves—belatedly.

13. For example, the Bernreuter (1933) personality questionnaire, the Guilford–Zimmerman inventory of temperament, the Minnesota Personality Inventory by Hathaway and MacKinley, or the 16 PF by R. B. Cattell and H. W. Eber.

14. At present, about a quarter of 20- to 25-year-old people are without work, contributing to a total unemployment level of more than 10 percent of the overall active population.

15. When the so-called school "of human relations" developed in the United States, we sometimes a little lightly thought it would be possible to improve the efficiency of companies by putting at the disposal of the personnel a psychologist whose main role would be to listen to any member of staff who desired it. Each one could then come to him to talk about his own personal problems or those linked to his surroundings in the company. It was thus hoped, by conducting the interview in a nondirective way, to help to solve, or at least reduce, personal and interpersonal conflicts. In the case of greater difficulties the counselor could only facilitate the clients decision to consult a psychotherapist and accept if required a program of therapy. The role of the neo-counselor as we propose it has only one thing in common with the counselor: he can help the normal subject to solve his own problems.

16. And not to start from the capacities and go toward the depth of the personality, which characterized classical guidance.

17. A conscious and accepted concession is no longer a loss of autonomy. If it remains unconscious at the moment of the decision it will be the source of later difficulties (reproaches, bitterness, etc.).

18. Consultants rather than counselors.

19. We have had the opportunity of hearing about two very recent experiments (unpublished) carried out in this way on unemployed workers who had to be retrained. It seems that the success rate over two years is better than 80 percent, whereas it hardly exceeds 20 percent when the usual method is followed.

REFERENCES

Bernreuter, R. G. 1933. The theory and construction of the Personality Inventory. *Journal of Social Psychology,* 4:387–405.

Goguelin, P. 1964. Goûts et aptitudes, *Le travail humain*, 3–4: 343–348.

Sinoir, G. 1943. *L'orientation professionnelle*. Paris: Presses Universitaires de France, n. 121.

10

Coping with Frustrations to Self-Realization: Stress, Anxiety, Crises, and Adjustment

Norman S. Endler & James D. A. Parker

This chapter is on individual self-realization and on some of the factors that may thwart the achievement of self-realization, factors such as crises, stress, anxiety, and vulnerability. Minimizing or coping with these factors may lead to adjustment and self-realization. All of us go through various stresses, crises, anxieties, and hassles throughout our lives. How we cope with these stresses and crises determines our level of adjustment and to what extent we self-actualize our potential for growth and development. Thus self-realization is an ongoing, lifelong developmental process.

The chapter reviews the major issues related to crises, stress, anxiety, and vulnerability, describing how each of these factors can influence self-realization. The chapter concludes with a discussion of several coping and adjustment strategies that have been found to be useful in dealing with frustrations to self-realization.

CRISES

Hirschowitz (1973) has defined a crisis as a "state of temporary disequilibrium precipitated by inescapable life change events." According to Bonkalo (1984), this definition of crisis emphasizes the temporary nature of situational conditions and the inescapable quality of the situation. This goes beyond recognizing that a series of events represents a potential or actual "turning point" in a person's life. Any crisis-induced imbalance often involves temporary conditions, because it can be corrected relatively early, often within a few weeks. Obviously, "the definition stipulates speed and ascribes little importance to the nature of the correction, whether the correction is regarded to be appropriate, or it is achieved by maladaptive means" (Bonkalo, 1984, p. 98). Usually the events have an inescapable quality, because for a *crisis* to occur a "no exit" situation is required. The individual feels trapped, according to Bonkalo (1984), because the situation cannot be avoided, and the context of situational events cannot usually be changed to a significant extent.

All of us go through a series of developmental stages or phases—critical for some, relatively easy to negotiate for others. For example, going off to kindergarten for the first time is an event that all children have to negotiate. For some children, especially those who have never been separated from their parents, this may induce separation anxiety and may present them (and their parents) with a crisis. However, if they have been inoculated against this potential trauma (i.e. if they have been to nursery school previously or if they have had this event simulated and explained to them), then they can negotiate this event without too much difficulty.

Similarly, going off to university in a strange town or city, or going to summer camp, finding one's first job, getting married, or having children are events that most of us have to negotiate, and hence they may present potential crises. Most of us resolve these "crises" without too much difficulty. How one resolves these events is a function of one's *vulnerability* (which is a function of previous experiences and temperamental and genetic factors), one's *perception of the situational crisis or stress*, the *interaction* of the two, and the *coping skills* that one has developed to cope with stress. Vulnerability, perception of stress, and coping mechanisms are all related to a person's self-concept, especially to his or her level of self-efficacy (see Bandura, 1986, for a discussion of the latter).

In addition to the crises that all of us encounter, and which we usually negotiate, there are crises that are unique to individuals, such as divorce or the premature death of a child or spouse. There are crises that are unique to groups of individuals, such as natural disasters (e.g. earthquakes, floods) or man-made disasters (e.g. terrorist attacks, nuclear disasters, war). These types of unique crises may be more difficult to resolve because we may not possess the experience and response repertoires for coping with them. The resolution of these crises (e.g. earthquakes, nuclear disasters) may not be under our control. However, a generalized level of self-efficacy reduces our stress and vulnerability and facilitates adjustment.

Different fears and different anxieties are prevalent at different ages and in different situations. Magnusson and his colleagues (Magnusson and Olah, 1981; Magnusson and Stattin, 1977; Stattin, 1983; Stattin and Magnusson, 1981) asked 12-, 15-, and 18-year-olds to describe three anxiety-provoking situations that came to mind. More than 20 percent of the 12-year-old *girls* reported archaic situations, achievement-demanding situations, self-situations, situations involving their parents, and situations involving threats by dangerous people. For 15- and 18-year-old *girls* the dominant type of situation is "demand for achievement and social evaluation". For *boys*, archaic, medical, and parent situations (presented more than 20 percent of the time at the age of 12) manifest a decreasing trend over the age span. At age 18 the most dominant type of anxiety-provoking situation for boys is "demand for achievement and social evaluation." There are also sex by age interactions with respect to anxiety-provoking situations.

Erikson (1963), Levinson (1978), and Sheehy (1976) have discussed stages of psychosocial development with regard to stage-related crises that need to be negotiated. The work of these researchers on aging has outlined some common features about adult development. There would appear to be types of crises that are more likely to occur at different times in an individual's life. Beginning with the very young adult, crises over intimacy become more likely than crises over identity. Later, crises over career decisions and issues increase in likelihood, as do conflicts centered around having children and raising a family. In later adulthood, crises surrounding death, or the "search for meaning" are increasingly more common. When studying the psychological effects of particular life events it is important to take into account the age of the individual, and the relationship between this event and other life events. The psychological impact of a life event is related to its timing and other relevant events, and the meaning of an event is influenced by its context and the person's life history (Elder and Rockwell, 1978).

Much of the research on the effects of stressful life events or adjustment and functioning has emphasized major, nonrecurring events, (e.g. birth, marriage, divorce, death). Most of the time, however, smaller and recurring stresses and disruptions are part of our daily existence. How frequently they occur, and how intensely they are perceived, may well be related to a decrement in psychological and physical functioning (see Edwards, 1984). Lazarus and his colleagues (Kanner, Coyne, Schaefer, and Lazarus, 1981) have noted the significance of small, daily life stresses, or "hassles." Developing a Hassles Scale, assessing the effects of such events as traffic jams, noise, the weather, insufficient time for family, shopping, Kanner et al. (1981) investigated the relationships among life events, hassles, and psychological symptoms. They found that hassles were a better predictor of psychological and physical symptoms than major life events. Hassles may have an impact on health and illness via their cumulative impact, or they may affect the relationship between illness and major life events. For example, if a major life-stress event (e.g. losing one's job) occurs at a time when there are few hassles, the stress may have fewer negative consequences than if a variety of hassles were present.

STRESS

Everyone is aware of the effects that stress can have on the individual's physical and psychological well-being. The concept of stress, as it is used in physiology and psychology, was borrowed from physics, where it was used to indicate a mechanical force acting on a body, with strain being the reaction to stress (Harris and Levey, 1975). Important, early work on stress in the life sciences was conducted by Selye (1956). The concept quickly became a very strong focus of theory and research (Appley and Trumbull, 1967; Endler and Edwards, 1988). Stress has become a general rubric term, with many related concepts, such as anxiety, conflict, and emotional distress encompassed under this construct (Appley and Trumbull, 1967).

Selye (1956) emphasized the physiological response and defined stress as a nonspecific response of the body to any demand. The initial research on stress life events, however, focused on the situation, primarily on the degree of change that had occurred in one's life (Holmes and Rahe, 1967). Stress definitions, primarily in terms of responses or situations, are usually inadequate in terms of research (cf. Dohrenwent and Dohrenwent, 1978; Goldberger and Breznitz, 1982; Rabkin and Struening, 1976). That is, no single response or family of responses are always indicative of stress. Furthermore, except for extreme life-threatening events, there appear to be no situations that are universal stressors. Disagreements have permeated attempts to define stress, either objectively or psychologically, and have generated an interest in interaction models of stress.

Spielberger (1976) has suggested that the stress construct has been used, historically, to refer to both *stressors* (dangerous or threatening stimulus conditions) that elicit anxiety reactions, and the *stress reactions* (cognitive, affective, behavioral, and physiological changes) that are elicited by the stressful stimuli. Spielberger goes on to suggest that the concepts of *stress* and *threat* should be used to identify different temporal phases of a process that produces an anxiety reaction. In this proposed model *stress* is used to identify the objective stimulus properties of a situation, while *threat* is used to refer to the perception of danger by an individual in the particular situation. In general, situations that are objectively stressful (e.g. earthquakes, loss of one's job) will be perceived as threatening. Nevertheless, as Spielberger has noted, "a stressful situation may not be perceived as threatening by an individual who either does not recognize the inherent danger, or has the necessary skills and experience to cope with it" (Spielberger, 1976, p. 5).

It frequently happens, however, that an objectively nonstressful situation may be perceived as dangerous by persons who appraise the situation as threatening for them. There are a number of factors that determine whether a situation will be perceived as personally threatening (Endler, 1988). These factors include the general mood of the person, the objective stimulus cues of the situation, the individual's previous experience with similar situations, and the cognitions and memories evoked by the current situation.

Coyne and Lazarus (1980) emphasize that stress should *not* be defined in terms of either the person *or* the situation, but rather as a transaction between person and situation. According to Lazarus and Folkman (1984), stress is a "particular relationship between the person and the environment that is appraised by the person as taxing his or her resources and endangering his or her wellbeing" (p. 19). Basically, stress refers to an interaction between the person and the environment which is perceived as taxing or exceeding the person's resources. Stressors refer to environmental variables that are potential sources of stress.

ANXIETY

Beginning with Freud (1933) and extending to the cognitive social learning theorists (Bandura, 1982, 1986), anxiety has been a major construct in most theories of personality and abnormal psychology. To explain the neuroses, Freud focused on anxiety and conflict. His neurotic process theories had a profound influence on the nomenclature and classification systems relevant to psychological disorders (Millon, 1984). Although Freud viewed anxiety as integral to the psychological development of each individual, it was difficult for psychologists to accept the concept of normal anxiety (May, 1950). In fact, it was not until the 1950s that "normal" anxiety became accepted in the psychiatric and psychological literature. Since that time, however, literally thousands of articles and books have been published on anxiety. Today, it is common for professionals and the lay public to consider anxiety an important and natural part of everyday experience.

Unfortunately, the concept of anxiety has been defined in a variety of inconsistent and contradictory ways. Anxiety has been used to refer to a stimulus, response, drive, motive, and trait (Endler, 1975). Spielberger (1972) has suggested that much conceptual confusion in the anxiety literature could be avoided if researchers distinguished between state anxiety and trait anxiety. State anxiety is defined as a reaction "consisting of unpleasant consciously-perceived feelings of tension and apprehension, with associated activation or arousal of the autonomic nervous system" (Spielberger, 1972, p. 29). Trait anxiety "refers to relatively stable individual differences in anxiety proneness, i.e., to differences among people in the disposition or tendency to perceive a wide range of situations as threatening and to respond to these situations with differential elevations in state anxiety" (Spielberger, 1975, p. 137).

Endler (1980, 1983) and Endler, Edwards, and Vitelli (in press) have proposed a multidimensional interaction model of anxiety. This model incorporates three important conceptual distinctions: (1) state and trait anxiety are distinct constructs; (2) state and trait anxiety are both multidimensional constructs; and (3) state anxiety is the product of an interaction between congruent dimensions of trait anxiety and situational stress.

Persons differ in anxiety proneness with respect to various dimensions of potentially anxiety-provoking situations (e.g. social evaluation, physical danger, ambiguous situations). To predict state anxiety one must take into account the specific dimension of trait anxiety and the type of threat in a stressful situation. An individual high on social evaluation trait anxiety is highly likely to experience an increase in state anxiety when encountering social evaluation situations (e.g. going for a job interview, or giving a talk). The interactional model of anxiety has important implications for the care and treatment of individuals experiencing psychological distress. Certain forms of therapeutic intervention may be more effective for individuals who experience high levels of anxiety in particular types of situations.

VULNERABILITY

Individuals differ in their perception of and reactions to the same objective stressors. Vulnerability is the term that is used to refer to these individual differences in susceptibility to stressors (cf. Garmezy, 1981). The interaction model of personality (Endler and Magnusson, 1976) states that personal individual differences interact with specific ranges or types of environments to influence behavior. A wide variety of individual differences may be implicated in determining a person's vulnerability to specific types or intensities of stressors. These differences in vulnerability may be cognitive, emotional, or motivational (Endler, 1983) and may result both from genetic differences (cf. Singer, 1984) and from learning, in interaction with a person's environment (cf. Chess, Thomas, and Birch, 1976).

Studies of natural and man-made disasters (Adams and Adams, 1984; Baum, Fleming, and Singer, 1982) suggest that there are transient and long-term responses to stress. These responses may include emotional reactions of anxiety, depression, anger, and feelings of helplessness, along with psychosomatic reactions. Individuals may also be vulnerable to a number of latent health problems. Adams and Adams (1984) studied a community located near Mount St. Helens, which erupted in May 1980. They found post-disaster stress reactions that included increases in illness, substance abuse, and violence. Individuals who experienced the dam collapse and flood near Buffalo Creek, West Virginia, suffered similar effects (Baum et al., 1982). It is important to note, however, that even more mundane naturally occurring events can have long-term implications. Burke, Borus, Burns, Millstein, and Beasley (1982) found that a relatively small-scale stressful event of a severe winter storm had considerable impact on the behavior of a group of children for many months afterwards.

ADJUSTMENT, CRISES, AND SELF-EFFICACY

As indicated earlier, there are crises that all of us negotiate during normal development, or what Erikson (1959) has called "development crises," and these are crises due to fortuitous events or what Erikson has called "accidental crises." How one negotiates these crises is a function of the interaction of learning, psychosocial, temperament, biological, and genetic factors. Success in coping with these crises facilitates adjustment; failure facilitates disorganization and maladjustment. Two factors that facilitate adjustment are discussed: (1) inoculation against stress and crises; and (2) self-efficacy.

Inoculation

Caplan (1964), in discussing the most frequent responses to crises, suggests that it might be possible to minimize the detrimental effects of developmental crises by a form of "psychological inoculation." This would involve some form of educational program that would be aimed at making persons realize that they are not unique in the developmental crises they have to negotiate. In a sense this is related to social comparison processes. If a child going off to kindergarten for his first time realizes that most of the other children feel somewhat uneasy about this experience, then the burden is easier to bear. If a Ph.D. candidate realizes that it is "perfectly normal" to experience some anxiety at an oral examination, this should tend to lessen his or her level of anxiety somewhat. If we learn what to expect at various stages of development, this can inoculate against crises and make us less vulnerable.

Of course there may be a number of factors that influence the effectiveness of this "inoculation." Kobasa (1979), for example, has postulated "hardiness" as a personality characteristic that distinguishes individuals who become ill or suffer emotional distress because of high levels of stress and those individuals who do not. Hardy individuals believe that they can *control* or influence stressful events they experience and possess the ability to feel strongly committed to their life activities. These individuals perceive change as an existing and challenging event. Change allows them to develop and grow as individuals. Kobasa's research, and the work of others studying business executives in highly stressful work environments, has found a consistent relationship between hardiness and illness (Kobasa, 1979; Kobasa, Maddi, and Kahn, 1982; Kobasa and Puccetti, 1983). Endler (1988, p. 39) suggests that "hardiness affects both appraisal of an event and coping strategies in negotiating that event. Hardiness, via cognitive appraisal, enables the person to transform a stressful experience into a less stressful form rather than avoiding the situation."

Thompson (1981), after reviewing the literature on control over stressful events and the degree of resulting psychological stress and discomfort, emphasized that when individuals believe they can control the administrations of a stressor, the stressor is perceived as less unpleasant than for individuals who do not believe they have control over the stressor. Thus the reaction to a potentially stressful event frequently depends on the meaning that event has for the individual. Goodhart (1985) found that "negative thinking about prior stressor outcomes appeared to increase vulnerability to the impact of later ones on several aspects of well being" (p. 216). Her research found that positive thinking, on the other hand, had minimal long-term effects. It was *not* the presence of positive thinking, but the *absence* of negative thinking, that was beneficial.

Scheier, Weintraub, and Carver (1986) found that "optimists" cope with stress better than "pessimists." They found that optimists react to disappointments and negative events (e.g. not getting into graduate school) by talking to other people and developing a plan of action to cope with the situation. On the other hand, pessimists react by "giving up" or attempting to forget about their rejections. Seligman (1981) has suggested that the manner in which individuals explain their successes and failures affects both their achievements and their psychological health. Pessimists view their failures, such as failing an examination, or losing out on a job promotion, as the result of personal deficiencies. Seligman believes that explanatory style may be changeable in response to important events in one's life. Evidence has been presented that suggests that explanatory style can be changed or modified through psychotherapy (Peterson and Seligman, 1987).

It has been suggested that educators, counselors and therapists consider "stress inoculation training" as important components for education and therapy programs (Kendall and Bemis, 1984). Individuals need to learn to develop and employ skills that enable them to cope with different types of stressful situations. The goal is to engender a sense of "learned resourcefulness" to counter the negative impact of feelings of "learned helplessness" (Kendall and Bemis, 1984).

Self-Efficacy

According to Bandura (1986), "among the different aspects of self-knowledge, perhaps none is more influential in people's everyday lives than conceptions of their personal-efficacy" (p. 390). Bandura (1986) emphasizes that "efficacy in dealing with one's environment is not simply a matter of knowing what to do" (p. 391). Self-efficacy involves a generative capacity "in which cognitive, social, and behavioral subskills must be organized into integrated courses of action to serve innumerable purposes" (Bandura, 1986, p. 391). Self-efficacy influences choice of behavior, the degree and persistence of our coping efforts, and our thoughts and emotional reactions to potential stressors (Bandura, 1986). Adjustment and competent functioning involve not only skills but self-perceptions or self-beliefs that one is efficacious. It has been found, for example, that the higher the level of perceived self-efficacy, the larger the number of career options the individual will consider. Higher levels of self-efficacy are also associated with more interest and enjoyment in particular careers (Bandura, 1986; Wheeler, 1983). Field studies with athletes have found that the higher the perceived self-efficacy, the better the performance. This result has been found with diverse activities such as track and field, tennis, and gymnastics (Bandura, 1986).

Self-efficacy is a lifelong process that involves interactions and reciprocal interrelationships of thoughts, perceptions, motivations, emotions, and actions. It is important to conduct longitudinal studies of persons, the situations they encounter, and how they cope with them (see Erikson, 1963; Levinson, 1978; Sheehy, 1976). It is also important to examine what situations make different people vulnerable and how efficacious people are in coping with their vulnerabilities.

CONCLUSIONS

Frustration, stress, anxiety, and crises are part and parcel of everyone's life, and the dynamic interrelationships of all these factors are highly complex. The development of adequate coping strategies to deal with frustrations, stress, anxiety, and crises will enhance adjustment and facilitate self-realization. Self-efficacy (Bandura, 1986), a belief in a person's ability to cope with specific situations, influences an individual's stress reactions and his/her consequent behavior (cf. Endler, 1988). Persons who are high in self-efficacy, and who develop strategies for controlling their lives (Seligman, 1985) and mastering life's problems, will lead better adjusted lives and will be able to focus on positive and creative aspects of their lives: a prerequisite for self-realization.

REFERENCES

Adams, P. R., and Adams, G. R. 1984. Mount Saint Helen's ashfall: Evidence for a disaster stress reaction. *American Psychologist*, 39: 252–260.

Appley, M. H., and Trumbull, R. 1967. *Psychological Stress: Issues in Research*. New York: Appleton-Century-Crofts.

Bandura, A. 1982. Self efficacy mechanism in human agency. *American Psychologist*, 37: 122–147.

Bandura, A. 1986. *Social Foundations of Thought and Action: A Social Cognitive Theory*. Englewood-Cliffs, N.J.: Prentice Hall.

Baum, A., Fleming, R., and Singer, J. E. 1982. Stress at Three Mile Island: Applying psychological impact analysis. In L. Bickman (Ed.), *Applied Social Psychology Annual*, Vol. 3. Beverly Hills, Calif.: Sage, pp. 217–248.

Bonkalo, A. 1984. Transient and situational disorders. In N. S.Endler and J.McV. Hunt (Eds.), *Personality and the Behavioral Disorders*, Vol. 2, 2nd ed. New York: John Wiley, pp. 897–913.

Burke, J. D., Borus, J. F., Burns, B. J., Millstein, J. H., and Beasley, M. C. 1982. Changes in children's behavior after a natural disaster. *American Journal of Psychiatry*, 139: 1010–1014.

Caplan, G. 1964. *Principles of Preventive Psychiatry*. New York: Basic Books.

Chess, S., Thomas, A., and Birch, H. G. 1976. Behavior problems revisited: Findings of an anterospective study. In N. S. Endler, L. R. Boulter, and H. Osser (Eds.), *Contemporary Issues in Development Psychology*, 2nd ed. New York: Holt, Rinehart and Winston, pp. 562–568.

Coyne, J. C., and Lazarus, R. S. 1980. Cognitive style, stress perception, and coping. In I. L. Kutash and L. B. Schlesinger (Eds.), *Handbook on Stress and Anxiety: Contemporary Knowledge, Theory and Treatment*. San Francisco, Calif.: Jossey-Bass Publishers, pp. 144–158.

Dohrenwend, B. S., and Dohrenwend, B. P. 1978. Some issues in research on stressful life events. *The Journal of Nervous and Mental Disease*, 166: 7–15.

Edwards, J. M. 1984. Situational determinants of behavior. In N. S. Endler and J. McV. Hunt (Eds.), *Personality and the Behavioral Disorders*, Vol. 1, 2nd ed. New York: John Wiley, pp. 147–182.

Elder, G. H. Jr., and Rockwell, R. C. 1978. The life-course and human development: An ecological perspective. *International Journal of Behavioural Development*, 2: 1–21.

Endler, N. S. 1975. A person–situation interaction model of anxiety. In C. D. Spielberger and I. G. Sarason (Eds.), *Stress and Anxiety*, Vol. 1. Washington, D.C.: Hemisphere/Wiley, pp. 145–164.

Endler, N. S. 1980. Person–situation interaction and anxiety. In I. L. Kutash and L. B. Schlesinger (Eds.), *Handbook on Stress and Anxiety: Contemporary Knowledge, Theory and Treatment*. San Francisco: Jossey-Bass, pp. 249–266.

Endler, N. S. 1983. Interactionism: A personality model, but not yet a theory. In M. M. Page (Ed.), *Nebraska Symposium on Motivation 1982. Personality—Current Theory and Research*. Lincoln, Nebraska: University of Nebraska Press, pp. 155–200.

Endler, N. S. 1988. Hassles, health and happiness. In M. P. Janisse (Ed.), *Individual Differences, Stress and Health Psychology*. New York: Springer, pp. 24–56.

Endler, N. S., and Edwards, J. M. 1988. Vulnerability and stress. In C. G. Last and M. Hersen (Eds.), *Handbook of Anxiety Disorders*. New York: Pergamon Press, pp. 141–169.

Endler, N. S., Edwards, J. M., and Vitelli, R. In press. *The Endler Multidimensional Anxiety Scale: Manual*. Los Angeles, Calif.: Western Psychological Services.

Endler, N. S., and Magnusson, D. 1976. Toward an interactional psychology of personality. *Psychological Bulletin*, 83: 956–974.

Erikson, E. 1959. *Identity and the Life Cycle*. Psychological Issues. Monograph 1, 1(1). New York: International Universities Press.

Erikson, E. H. 1963. *Childhood and Society*, 2nd ed. New York: Norton.

Freud, S. 1933. *New Introductory Lectures on Psychoanalysis*. New York: Norton.

Garmezy, N. 1981. Children under stress: Perspectives on antecedents and correlates of vulnerability and resistance to psychopathology. In A. I. Rabin, L. Aronoff, A. M. Barclay, and R. A. Zucker (Eds.), *Further Explorations in Personality*. New York: John Wiley and Sons, pp. 126–269.

Goldberger, L., and Breznitz, S. (Eds.). 1982. *Handbook of Stress*. New York: Free Press/MacMillan.

Goodhart, D. E. 1985. Some psychological effects associated with positive and negative thinking about stressful event outcomes: Was Pollyanna right? *Journal of Personality and Social Psychology*, 48: 216–232.

Harris, W. H., and Levey, J. S. (Eds.) 1975. *The New Columbia Encyclopedia*, 4th ed. New York: Columbia University Press.

Hirschowitz, R. G. 1973. Crisis theory: A formulation. *Psychiatric Annals*, 3: 33–47.

Holmes, T. H., and Rahe, R. H. 1967. The Social Readjustment Rating Scale. *Journal of Psychosomatic Research*, 11: 213–218.

Kanner, A. D., Coyne, J. C., Schaefer, C., and Lazarus, R. S. 1981. Comparison of two modes of stress measurement: Daily hassles and uplifts versus major life events. *Journal of Behavioral Medicine*, 4: 1–39.

Kendall, P. C., and Bemis, K. M. 1984. Cognitive behavioral interventions: Principles and procedures. In N. S. Endler and J. McV. Hunt (Eds.), *Personality and the Behavioral Disorders*, Vol. 2, 2nd ed., pp. 1069–1109.

Kobasa, S. C. 1979. Stressful life events, personality, and health: An inquiry into hardiness. *Journal of Personality and Social Psychology*, 37: 1–11.

Kobasa, S. C., Maddi, S. R., and Kahn, S. 1982. Hardiness and health: A prospective study. *Journal of Personality and Social Psychology*, 42: 168–177.

Kobasa, S. C., and Puccetti, M. C. 1983. Personality and social resources in stress resistance. *Journal of Personality and Social Psychology*, 45: 839–850.

Lazarus, R. S., and Folkman, S. 1984. *Stress, Appraisal and Coping*. New York: Springer Publishing.

Levinson, D. J. 1978. *The Seasons of a Man's Life*. New York: Knopf.

Magnusson, D., and Olah, A. 1981. Situation–outcome contingencies: A study of anxiety provoking situations in a developmental perspective. *Results from the Department of Psychology, University of Stockholm, No. 574.*

Magnusson, D., and Stattin, H. 1977. Cross-national comparisons of anxiousness employing a Situation by Reaction Inventory—IRS-1. *Reports from the Department of Psychology, University of Stockholm, No. 506.*

May, R. 1950. *The Meaning of Anxiety*. New York: Ronald Press.

Millon, L. 1984. The DSM III: Some historical and substantive reflections. In N. S. Endler and J. McV. Hunt (Eds.), *Personality and the Behavioral Disorders*, Vol. 2, 2nd ed., pp. 675–710.

Peterson, C., and Seligman, M. E. P. 1987. Explanatory styles and illness. *Journal of Personality*, 55: 237–266.

Rabkin, J. G., and Struening, E. L. 1976. Life events, stress, and illness. *Science*, 194: 1013–1020.

Scheier, M. F., Weintraub, J. K., and Carver, C. S. 1986. Coping with stress: Divergent strategies of optimists and pessimists. *Journal of Personality and Social Psychology*, 51: 1257–1264.

Seligman, M. E. P. 1981. A learned helplessness point of view. In L. P. Rehm (Ed.), *Behavior Therapy for Depression: Present Status and Future Directions*. New York: Academic Press, pp. 123–141.

Selye, H. 1956. *The Stress of Life*. New York: McGraw-Hill.

Sheehy, G. 1976. *Passages*. New York: Dutton.

Singer, J. L. 1984. *The Human Personality*. New York: Harcourt, Brace, Jovanovich.

Spielberger, C. D. 1972. Anxiety as an emotional state. In C. D. Spielberger (Ed.), *Anxiety: Current Trends in Theory and Research*, Vol. 1. New York: Academic Press, pp. 24–49.

Spielberger, C. D. 1975. Anxiety: State–trait process. In C. D. Spielberger and I. G. Sarason (Eds.), *Stress and Anxiety*, Vol. 1. New York: John Wiley & Sons, pp. 115–143.

Spielberger, C. D. 1976. The nature and measurement of anxiety. In C. D. Spielberger and R. Diaz-Guerrero (Eds.), *Cross-Cultural Anxiety*. Washington, D.C.: Hemisphere, pp. 3–12.

Stattin, H. 1983. Developmental trends in the appraisal of anxiety provoking situations. *Reports from the Department of Psychology, University of Stockholm, No. 601.*

Stattin, H., and Magnusson, D. 1981. Situation-outcome contingencies of threatening experiences: Age and sex differences. *Reports from the Department of Psychology, University of Stockholm, No. 580.*

Thompson, S. C. 1981. Will it hurt less if I can control it? A complex answer to a simple question. *Psychological Bulletin*, 90: 89–101.

Wheeler, K. G. 1983. Comparisons of self-efficacy and expectancy models of occupational preferences for college males and females. *Journal of Occupational Psychology*, 56: 73–78.

Index

Contributors

Edgar Krau is Professor in the Department of Psychology and the Department of Labor Studies, Tel Aviv University, Israel. He received his Ph.D. in 1964 at the University of Cluj, Roumania. He taught until 1977 at the University of Cluj (Roumania), between 1977–1981 at the Haifa University (Israel), and since 1981 at Tel Aviv University. His main research interest is the psychology of vocational and social adjustment. In this area he has written more than 60 publications, which appeared in the United States and in several European countries.

Prof. Nancy E. Betz, Ph.D., Ohio State University, Columbus, Ohio, America.

Roland Capel, M.A. in natural science, M.A. in social and psychopedagogical sciences, Lausanne University, Switzerland.

Prof. Jean-Blaise Dupont, Ph.D. Lausanne University, Switzerland.

Prof. Norman S. Endler, Ph.D., York University, Ontario, Canada.

Prof. Pierre L. G. Goguelin, Ph.D., Conservatoire National des Arts et Métiers, Paris, France.

Claire Jobin, M.A. in sociology, M.A. in applied psychology, Lausanne University, Switzerland.

Prof. Abraham K. Korman, Ph.D., Distinguished Professor, Baruch College, City University of New York, America.

James D. A. Parker, M.A. in psychology, York University, Ontario, Canada.

Prof. Bernhard Wilpert, Ph.D., Berlin University of Technology, Berlin, Federal Republic of Germany.